STECK-VAUGHN

TARGET Spelling 780

Margaret Scarborough
Mary F. Brigham
Teresa A. Miller

STECK-VAUGHN
COMPANY

Table of Contents

About the Authors

Margaret M. Scarborough teaches at Elizabeth Seawell Elementary School in Chapel Hill, North Carolina. Her master's degree was conferred by the University of North Carolina. Ms. Scarborough has taught kindergarten through sixth-grade students with special learning needs. She works collaboratively with regular classroom teachers, remedial reading teachers, speech and language pathologists, and behavioral therapists. She is a member of the Learning Disabilities Association of North Carolina and past president of the Orange County Association for Children and Adults with Learning Disabilities.

Mary F. Brigham is principal of McNair Elementary School in Fort Bragg, North Carolina. She has led language arts, early childhood, and remedial reading programs for the Fort Bragg Schools, in addition to having had varied teaching experience at all levels. Ms. Brigham earned her master's degree at the University of North Carolina at Chapel Hill, where she is currently enrolled in the doctoral program in educational administration.

Teresa A. Miller has taught children in Virginia, Vermont, and North Carolina. Her degrees in education are from the College of William and Mary, and the University of North Carolina at Chapel Hill. She has worked with both children and adults in a wide variety of educational settings.

Acknowledgments
Cover Design: Sharon Golden, James Masch
Cover Illustration: Terrell Powell
Interior Design and Production: Dodson Publication Services
Illustrators: Peg Dougherty, Jimmy Longacre

Staff Credits
Executive Editor: Elizabeth Strauss
Project Editor: Chris Boyd
Project Manager: Sharon Golden

Words with *er*

her	jerk	perch	herd
fern	nerve	verb	perk

A. Fill in each blank with a spelling word.

1. She feels sick, so I took _____ some soup.

2. A _____ is a nice plant to grow.

3. It takes _____ to be a firefighter.

4. The bird is sitting on its _____.

5. The carnival ride made me _____ from side to side.

6. An action word is called a _____.

7. The coffee is about to _____.

8. A _____ of wild horses could not drag me away!

B. Circle the word that is the same as the top one.

<u>her</u>	<u>fern</u>	<u>jerk</u>	<u>nerve</u>	<u>perch</u>	<u>verb</u>	<u>herd</u>	<u>perk</u>
him	fenn	jerk	rerve	porch	werb	berd	perk
hen	fenr	jark	nirve	perch	verd	herd	pork
yer	fern	jarh	narve	qerch	verb	herb	park
(her)	tarn	yerk	nerve	pench	vorb	harb	qerk

C. Write a spelling word under each picture.

1. _____ 2. _____ 3. _____

Name _____

Words with *er*

her	jerk	perch	herd
fern	nerve	verb	perk

A. Fill in the boxes with the right words.

1.

2.

3.

4.

5.

6.

B. Write the spelling words that rhyme with the words below.

1. turn   learn   _____

2. curve   swerve   _____

3. lurk   perk   _____

4. bird   word   _____

C. Write the correct spelling word beside each clue.

fern _____ 1. a plant that likes wet places

_____ 2. courage

_____ 3. goes with "she"

_____ 4. a pole or rod for a bird

_____ 5. many animals in a group

_____ 6. to jump up or become lively

_____ 7. a quick, sharp pull or twist

_____ 8. a word that shows action

Words with *er*

her	jerk	perch	herd
fern	nerve	verb	perk

A. Find the missing letters. Then write the word.

1. v ___ ___ b   _____

2. n ___ r v ___   _____

B. Write the spelling words in alphabetical (ABC) order.

1. _____ 2. _____ 3. _____ 4. _____

5. _____ 6. _____ 7. _____ 8. _____

C. Use spelling words to complete the story.

The cowboys who went on trail drives years ago are the real heroes of the West. They would move a _____ of cattle from the South to the North. Most trails ended in Kansas. There the beef from the herd was sent east by rail.

Trail drives were full of danger and lasted for months. The weather would turn bad, and thieves would try to steal herds. At night, one cowboy would _____ on his horse to watch for thieves while the others slept.

It took _____ to be a cowboy on trail drives.

D. Finish the sentences.

1. It's <u>her</u> turn to _____.

2. The <u>fern</u> I bought is _____.

© 1991 Steck-Vaughn Company. Target 780

Name_____

Words with *er*

her	jerk	perch	herd
fern	nerve	verb	perk

A. Complete these exercises with spelling words.

1. Write the words that begin with *per*.

_____   _____

2. Write the words that begin with *h*.

_____   _____

3. Write the word that ends with a vowel. _____

B. Use spelling words to answer these riddles.

1. This is a sharp pull, push, or bounce.

What is it? _____

2. This is the courage you need to take a test. It also names a type of fiber in your body.

What is it? _____

3. Birds like to sit on this. It can also be a kind of fish.

What is it? _____

C. Use each spelling word in a sentence.

herd _____

nerve _____

perk _____

fern _____

verb _____

Words with *ur*

burst	burn	church	purse
turn	nurse	curve	curb

A. Fill in each blank with a spelling word.

1. The wedding was held in the _____.

2. I met a very nice _____ in the hospital.

3. It's my _____ to do the dishes.

4. The balloon _____ from too much air.

5. When a line bends, it's called a _____.

6. Don't _____ your hand on the hot stove.

7. We stood on the _____ before crossing the street.

8. How much money do you have in your _____?

B. Circle the letters that are the same in all the words.

burst   turn   burn   nurse   church   curve   purse   curb

C. Write the spelling words that rhyme with the words below.

1. first   thirst   _____

2. fern   churn   _____

3. verse   worse   _____

4. search   perch   _____

5. herb   verb   _____

D. Finish the sentence.

The balloon <u>burst</u> _____.

© 1991 Steck-Vaughn Company. Target 780

Name _____

5

Words with *ur*

burst	burn	church	purse
turn	nurse	curve	curb

A. Circle the word that is the same as the top one.

burst	turn	burn	nurse	church	curve	purse	curb
burst	tunn	durn	nnrse	church	carve	qurse	carb
bursh	tunr	burn	nurse	cburch	cnrve	porse	curd
burts	furn	barn	narse	charch	curve	parse	curb
burns	turn	bunn	nunse	chorch	corve	purse	cunb

B. Complete these exercises with spelling words.

1. Which word means "to explode or break open"? _____

2. Which word means "a house of worship"? _____

3. Which word means "the edge of a street"? _____

4. Which word means "to be on fire"? _____

5. Which word means "a bending line"? _____

C. Fill in the boxes with the right words.

1.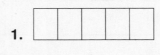

2.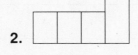

3.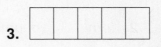

4.

5.

6.

D. Write the words that name things you can touch.

1. _____   2. _____   3. _____

4. _____   5. _____   6. _____

6

Words with *ur*

burst	burn	church	purse
turn	nurse	curve	curb

A. Use two of the spelling words in sentences.

1. _____

2. _____

B. Use spelling words to complete the story.

This is what happened the first time I called for a cab. I was waiting in front of my house. Soon I saw the cab come around a _____. Then it made a sharp _____ to miss hitting a dog. The taxi ran over the _____ and into the wall of a _____.

The minister _____ out of the church. "Are you all right?" he asked the driver.

"I'm fine," said the driver. "I'm sorry I hit your church."

The dog was all right, too. I was glad no one was hurt.

C. Write the spelling words in alphabetical order.

1. _____ 2. _____ 3. _____ 4. _____

5. _____ 6. _____ 7. _____ 8. _____

D. Write the spelling words that have five letters.

_____   _____

_____   _____

Name _____

Words with *ur*

burst	burn	church	purse
turn	nurse	curve	curb

A. One word is wrong in each sentence. Circle the wrong word. Then fill in the blank with a spelling word that makes sense.

1. The clown gave me a shot in the arm. _____

2. The balloon cried from having too much air. _____

3. You light a match to get a fire to walk. _____

4. She keeps her wallet in her garden. _____

B. Write a spelling word under each picture.

1. _____   2. _____   3. _____

C. Complete these exercises with spelling words.

1. Which word begins and ends with the same sound?

_____

2. Which words end with silent *e*?

_____   _____   _____

3. Which words have the letter *b* in them?

_____   _____   _____

4. Which words end in *urn*?

_____   _____

8

Words with *au*

launch	vault	fault	haunt
gauze	haul	cause	August

A. Fill in each blank with a spelling word.

1. Please put my money in the bank's _____.

2. We need to _____ away all the trash.

3. The car wreck was all my _____.

4. The U.S. Navy is going to _____ a new ship.

5. What was the _____ of the fire?

6. You wrap a burn in a _____ bandage.

7. A ghost may _____ you in this old house.

8. _____ is the eighth month of the year.

B. Find the missing letters. Then write the word.

1. v ___ ___ l t   _____

2. ___ ___ g u s t   _____

C. Circle the letters that are the same in all the words.

launch   gauze   vault   haul   fault   cause   haunt   August

D. Write the spelling words in alphabetical order.

1. _____   2. _____   3. _____   4. _____

5. _____   6. _____   7. _____   8. _____

Name _____

Words with *au*

launch	vault	fault	haunt
gauze	haul	cause	August

A. Use spelling words to complete the story.

Have you ever seen the _____ of a rocket? We saw one

launched last _____. It was the best part of my summer. If you

think a rocket looks big on TV, you should see the real thing!

It takes a few days just to _____ a rocket to the launch pad.

When it takes off, the power and noise _____ the ground to rumble

and shake.

B. Match each spelling word with the right clue.

_____ 1. haunt   **a.** to send off or set in motion

_____ 2. vault   **b.** what ghosts do

_____ 3. gauze   **c.** a room in a bank

_____ 4. launch   **d.** a piece of cloth used in first aid

_____ 5. haul   **e.** the name of a month

_____ 6. August   **f.** blame

_____ 7. fault   **g.** to carry

_____ 8. cause   **h.** something that brings about a result

C. Write the words that name things you cannot touch.

1. _____ 2. _____ 3. _____

4. _____ 5. _____ 6. _____

Words with *au*

launch	vault	fault	haunt
gauze	haul	cause	August

A. Circle the word that is the same as the top one.

launch	gauze	vault	haul	fault	cause	haunt	August
luanch	gouze	vault	baul	tault	couse	haunt	Aagust
lauuch	gauze	vaulf	hual	faulf	cause	baunt	Augusf
launch	pauze	voult	haul	fualt	cauze	haunf	August
leunch	guaze	wault	houl	fault	cuase	hount	Aujust

B. Write the spelling words that rhyme with the words below.

1. laws   saws   _____

2. fall   call   _____

3. malt   salt   _____

4. want   jaunt   _____

C. Use each spelling word in a sentence.

launch _____

gauze _____

vault _____

haul _____

fault _____

cause _____

haunt _____

August _____

Name _____

Words with *au*

launch	vault	fault	haunt
gauze	haul	cause	August

A. Find the hidden words on the list.

launch   vault   fault   haunt
gauze   haul   cause   August
law   draw   how   plow

```
u r l a u n c h m y l b e s t h f
r i e u n d w h y d a o n d r a w
t w v g a u z e h o w e g o o u t
t f a u l t o s a w i m o r g l o
f o u s r a c a u r r i d e i n y
o u l t r n e w n l i t p l o w t
l e t s p o r t t s c a u s e c o
u l d h a v e a l o t o f f u n i
```

B. Complete these exercises with spelling words.

1. Which word begins with a capital letter? _____

2. Which words end with a silent *e*?

   _____   _____

3. Which words begin with the same first letter?

   _____   _____

4. Which words end with *ult*?

   _____   _____

5. Which word ends with *ch*?

   _____

Homonyms

red	not	maid	be
read	knot	made	bee

A. Fill in each blank with a spelling word.

1. I _____ about you in the newspaper.

2. Can you tie a _____ in the rope?

3. The _____ will clean up our hotel room.

4. She _____ me a great birthday cake.

5. I am _____ going to do that for you.

6. When the light turns _____, you have to stop.

7. Will you _____ my valentine?

8. A _____ stung me on my foot.

B. Find the missing letters. Then write the word.

1. m ___ ___ d   _____

2. m ___ ___ e   _____

3. r ___ ___ d   _____

4. ___ ___ ___ t   _____

C. Write a spelling word under each picture.

1. _____   2. _____   3. _____

Name _____

Homonyms

red	not	maid	be
read	knot	made	bee

A. Fill in the boxes with the right words.

1.
2.
3.
4.

5.
6.
7.
8.

B. Match each spelling word with the right clue.

_____ **1.** knot   **a.** what you do with a book

_____ **2.** maid   **b.** caused something to be or to happen

_____ **3.** read   **c.** something tied together, or a tangle

_____ **4.** bee   **d.** the color of blood

_____ **5.** made   **e.** an insect that makes honey

_____ **6.** red   **f.** the homonym for "made"

C. Use spelling words to complete the story.

My aunt was hanging out clothes on the line, when a _____

stung her.

"Ouch!" she cried. She ran inside, holding her arm. The bee's sting

_____ a big purple and _____ knot.

She found a first-aid book and _____ that you should try to

_____ calm, get the stinger out, and put medicine on it. After my

aunt did that, she felt much better.

LESSON 4   Homonyms

red	not	maid	be
read	knot	made	bee

A. Complete these exercises with spelling words.

1. Write the words that end with *d*.

_____   _____   _____

2. Write the word that ends with two *e*'s. _____

3. Write the words that have the letter *o*.

_____   _____

B. Write the spelling words that rhyme with the words below.

1. paid   raid   _____

2. lot   cot   _____

3. see   me   _____

4. led   bed   _____

C. Use each spelling word in a sentence.

red   _____

read   _____

not   _____

knot   _____

maid   _____

made   _____

be   _____

bee   _____

Name _____

Homonyms

red	not	maid	be
read	knot	made	bee

A. Find the hidden words on the list.

red	not	maid	be
read	knot	made	bee
oil	spoil	coin	join

i	l	l	n	i	t	r	a	i	n	o	r	b	e	e	w	i	l
i	s	p	o	i	l	t	s	o	n	o	w	o	r	c	i	s	i
g	o	i	t	n	g	t	o	i	d	o	a	n	j	o	i	n	y
h	i	n	g	d	i	f	f	l	e	m	r	e	n	i	t	t	o
b	e	a	y	c	a	n	i	h	e	a	l	p	y	n	o	u	w
t	h	y	r	e	a	d	o	u	r	i	b	a	g	g	a	g	e
w	o	u	e	l	d	l	o	v	e	d	t	o	h	a	v	e	a
i	g	t	d	i	p	w	h	e	n	c	a	k	n	o	t	n	y
u	c	o	m	e	o	m	a	d	e	v	e	r	t	o	s	e	e
e	w	w	c	a	n	h	a	v	e	l	o	t	s	o	f	f	u

B. Write the spelling words in alphabetical order.

1. _____ 2. _____ 3. _____ 4. _____

5. _____ 6. _____ 7. _____ 8. _____

C. Complete these exercises with spelling words.

1. Write the word that names a color. _____

2. Write the word that starts with a silent letter. _____

3. Write the word that names a flying insect. _____

4. Write the word that has only two letters. _____

Words with *aw*

crawl	dawn	brawl	flaw
lawn	yawn	claw	straw

A. Fill in each blank with a spelling word.

1. The ranch hands had a _____ and broke all the chairs, tables, and dishes.

2. People _____ when they are tired.

3. Do you help mow the _____?

4. My brother wakes up at the crack of _____.

5. I had to _____ on the floor to find my glasses.

6. A mistake in something is called a _____.

7. My new hat is made out of _____.

8. The cat's _____ got hung on the wire.

B. Write the words that end in *aw*.

_____   _____   _____

C. Fill in the boxes with the right words.

1.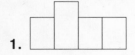

2.

3.

4.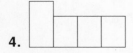

5.

6.

7.

8.

Name _____

Words with *aw*

crawl	dawn	brawl	flaw
lawn	yawn	claw	straw

A. Circle the word that is the same as the top one.

crawl	lawn	dawn	yawn	brawl	claw	flaw	straw
craml	lown	bawn	yawn	braml	clow	flow	strow
crawl	lamn	dawn	gawn	drawl	claw	flam	sfraw
cnawl	lawn	down	yown	brawl	clam	falw	straw
crowl	lewn	bamn	yawr	browl	clau	flaw	srtaw

B. Write the spelling words in alphabetical order.

1. _____   2. _____   3. _____   4. _____

5. _____   6. _____   7. _____   8. _____

C. Match each spelling word with the right clue.

_____ 1. dawn   **a.** a thin tube to drink through

_____ 2. yawn   **b.** what babies do before they walk

_____ 3. crawl   **c.** a fight

_____ 4. brawl   **d.** what people do when they are tired

_____ 5. lawn   **e.** the first light of the morning

_____ 6. claw   **f.** a mistake

_____ 7. flaw   **g.** a sharp nail on a cat's paw

_____ 8. straw   **h.** the part of a yard that is usually mowed

Words with *aw*

crawl	dawn	brawl	flaw
lawn	yawn	claw	straw

A. Find the missing letters. Then write the word.

1. c r ___ ___ ___   _____

2. s t ___ ___ ___   _____

B. Write a spelling word under each picture.

1. _____   2. _____   3. _____

C. Write the spelling words that rhyme with the words below.

1. lawn   yawn   _____

2. flaw   straw   _____

3. drawl   brawl   _____

D. Circle the letters that are the same in all the words.

crawl   lawn   dawn   yawn   brawl   claw   flaw   straw

E. Finish the sentences.

1. We had to <u>crawl</u> _____.

2. I woke up at <u>dawn</u> and _____.

3. He found a <u>flaw</u> in _____.

Name _____   **19**

LESSON 5

1
2
3
4

Words with *aw*

crawl	dawn	brawl	flaw
lawn	yawn	claw	straw

A. Use spelling words to complete the story.

I awoke at _____ to a chorus of terrible sounds. There was

hissing and spitting and growling and yowling. Two cats were having a

_____. I had never heard such a racket before! I jumped out of bed

and ran downstairs.

I grabbed a broom made of _____ and went outside to stop the

fight. The cats were on my front _____. They turned to look at me.

Then one cat tried to _____ the other. I ran at them with the broom.

Both cats sped out of my yard.

I saw one _____ under a house. The other cat ran down the street.

What a way to start a new day!

B. Use each spelling word in a sentence.

crawl _____

lawn _____

dawn _____

yawn _____

brawl _____

claw _____

flaw _____

straw _____

20

Words with *oo*

foot	wood	stood	crook
hook	brook	hood	cook

A. Fill in each blank with a spelling word.

1. We waded in the water of the little _____.

2. Let's bring some _____ in for the fire.

3. You have to put bait on the _____ to catch a fish.

4. I _____ up to see my team score.

5. The _____ of a car covers the engine.

6. He fell down and broke his _____.

7. The _____ burned the food.

8. The curved part of an umbrella handle is called a _____.

B. Find the missing letters. Then write the word.

1. s t ___ ___ d   _____

2. c ___ ___ ___ k   _____

C. Circle the letters that are the same in all the words.

foot   hook   wood   brook   stood   hood   crook   cook

D. One word is wrong in each sentence. Circle the wrong word. Then fill in the blank with a spelling word that makes sense.

1. I caught the fish on a toothpick.   _____

2. We need water to make the fire burn.   _____

3. You should thank the plate for the food we ate.   _____

4. We all flew up when our team scored.   _____

Name _____

Words with *oo*

| foot | wood | stood | crook |
| hook | brook | hood | cook |

A. Circle the word that is the same as the top one.

foot	hook	wood	brook	stood	hood	crook	cook
foof	book	mood	bnook	sfood	hood	cnook	dook
feet	hook	woob	breek	stood	heed	crook	beek
toof	heek	wood	drook	stoob	hoob	creek	booh
foot	hooh	weed	brook	steed	bood	croak	cook

B. Write the spelling words that rhyme with the words below.

1. hook   crook   _____

2. soot   put   _____

3. hood   stood   _____

4. brook   cook   _____

5. wood   hood   _____

C. Write the words that name things you can touch.

1. _____ 2. _____ 3. _____

4. _____ 5. _____ 6. _____

7. _____

D. Write the spelling words in alphabetical order.

1. _____ 2. _____ 3. _____ 4. _____

5. _____ 6. _____ 7. _____ 8. _____

Words with *oo*

foot	wood	stood	crook
hook	brook	hood	cook

A. Use spelling words to complete the story.

I went fishing last week with my friend. We _____ beside a little

_____ to catch the fish. We were going to _____ what we

caught.

I cast out my line and caught a big fish. I was pulling the _____

out of the fish's mouth when my _____ slipped. The fish flew out of

my hand and into the water. There went our supper!

B. Write a spelling word under each picture.

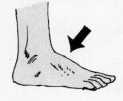  

1. _____ 2. _____ 3. _____

C. Complete these exercises with spelling words.

1. Write the words that end with *ook*.

_____   _____

_____   _____

2. Write the words that end with *ood*.

_____   _____   _____

3. Write the word that ends with a *t*.

_____

Name _____

Words with *oo*

foot	wood	stood	crook
hook	brook	hood	cook

A. Find the hidden words on the list.

foot	brook	crook	proud
hook	stood	cook	ground
wood	hood	cloud	pound

```
l  e  t  s  g  o  p  f  l  y  a  k  i  t  e  u  p  w
h  e  f  r  e  t  o  h  h  e  a  i  w  o  o  d  r  i
s  l  o  i  p  g  u  h  o  t  o  h  l  e  t  s  g  c
o  f  o  l  r  y  n  a  o  k  i  t  b  e  w  h  a  o
t  a  t  w  o  o  d  n  k  d  e  r  r  f  u  l  p  o
e  r  s  o  u  n  b  a  r  b  s  t  o  o  d  a  r  k
a  i  s  s  d  h  h  e  i  s  k  i  o  n  d  a  n  d
u  n  d  e  r  s  o  t  c  r  o  o  k  a  n  d  i  n
g  a  n  d  i  w  o  a  g  r  o  u  n  d  n  t  m  y
c  h  c  l  o  u  d  i  l  d  r  e  n  t  o  b  e  l
```

B. Use each spelling word in a sentence.

hook _____

wood _____

brook _____

C. Change one letter in each word to make a new word.

_____ **1.** Change "brook" to something you read.

_____ **2.** Change "foot" to what an owl says.

_____ **3.** Change "hook" to the name of a person who fixes food.

Words with *oo*

food	bloom	booth	goose
noon	loose	tooth	proof

A. Fill in each blank with a spelling word.

1. The flowers are ready to _____.

2. Superman changes clothes in a phone _____.

3. I lost weight, and now my clothes are too _____.

4. The _____ he cooks is really great!

5. Her _____ got knocked out in the hockey game.

6. Let's eat lunch today at 12 _____.

7. There is _____ that Earth is round.

8. A _____ looks like a big duck.

B. Circle the letters that are the same in all the words.

food   noon   bloom   loose   booth   tooth   goose   proof

C. Use spelling words to complete the story.

I sold flowers at our county fair. I rented a _____ and set up a

sign. At _____ the crowds arrived. Most of the booths sold

_____.

A _____ in the booth next to mine got _____ and ate

some of my flowers. Then somebody bought the goose. I sold a lot of

flowers, but I used most of my money to buy food at the fair.

Name _____

25

LESSON 7 Words with *oo*

food	bloom	booth	goose
noon	loose	tooth	proof

A. Circle the word that is the same as the top one.

food	noon	bloom	loose	booth	tooth	goose	proof
foob	gnoo	dloom	loose	booht	booth	goose	groof
feed	nune	bloow	leese	dooth	tooth	joose	proot
tood	noon	bloom	loase	booth	footh	geese	proof
food	soon	bleem	looes	beeth	thoot	gooes	pnoof

B. Write the spelling words in alphabetical order.

1. _____ 2. _____ 3. _____ 4. _____

5. _____ 6. _____ 7. _____ 8. _____

C. Match each spelling word with the right clue.

_____ 1. noon   **a.** an animal that makes a honking sound

_____ 2. goose   **b.** what we eat to stay alive

_____ 3. tooth   **c.** the place where people vote

_____ 4. food   **d.** one of the things you chew with

_____ 5. booth   **e.** lunchtime

_____ 6. loose   **f.** the flower on a plant

_____ 7. bloom   **g.** what you use to prove something

_____ 8. proof   **h.** the opposite of tight

26

Words with *oo*

food	bloom	booth	goose
noon	loose	tooth	proof

A. Find the missing letters. Then write the word.

1. __ __ o n   _____

2. b l __ __ __   _____

B. Use spelling words to complete the puzzle.

Across

2. Flowers ___ in spring.

4. The boy lost a ___.

6. not tight

7. what we eat

Down

1. lunchtime

2. a stall at a fair

3. It looks like a duck.

5. evidence

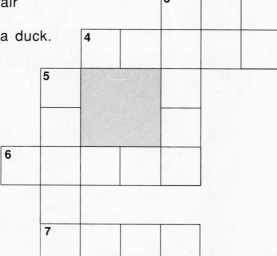

Name _____

LESSON 7

Words with *oo*

food	bloom	booth	goose
noon	loose	tooth	proof

A. Fill in the boxes with the right words.

1.

2.

3.

4.

5.

6.

7.

8.

B. Write a spelling word under each picture.

1. _____

2. _____

3. _____

C. Use each spelling word in a sentence.

food _____

noon _____

bloom _____

loose _____

booth _____

tooth _____

goose _____

proof _____

Words with *ie*

thief	niece	field	brief
chief	piece	shield	yield

A. Fill in each blank with a spelling word.

1. Who is the _____ of police?

2. Your brother's daughter is your _____.

3. An umbrella will _____ you from the rain.

4. A farmer plants crops in a _____.

5. I would love a _____ of cake.

6. The _____ ran off with my purse.

7. The yellow, three-sided sign means to _____.

8. She told us a _____ story, and then we left early.

B. Write the spelling words that rhyme with the words below.

1. shield   yield   _____

2. chief   brief   _____

3. geese   piece   _____

C. Write the words that name things you can touch.

1. _____   2. _____   3. _____

4. _____   5. _____   6. _____

D. Finish the sentences.

1. I saw a <u>field</u> of _____.

2. May I have a <u>piece</u> of _____?

Words with *ie*

thief	niece	field	brief
chief	piece	shield	yield

A. **Write a spelling word under each picture.**

1. _____ 2. _____ 3. _____

B. **Match each spelling word with the right clue.**

_____ **1.** brief   **a.** an open land area often used for planting crops

_____ **2.** yield   **b.** the leader of a group or tribe

_____ **3.** field   **c.** a sign that means slow down and let others go first

_____ **4.** shield   **d.** a person who steals

_____ **5.** piece   **e.** your sister's daughter

_____ **6.** thief   **f.** a part or a bit of something

_____ **7.** chief   **g.** something that is short or doesn't take much time

_____ **8.** niece   **h.** something that protects you

C. **Circle the letters that are the same in all the words.**

thief   chief   niece   piece   field   shield   brief   yield

D. **Find the missing letters. Then write the word.**

s __ __ __ l __   _____

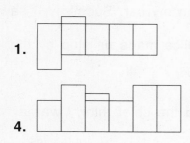

LESSON 8

Words with *ie*

thief	niece	field	brief
chief	piece	shield	yield

A. Fill in the boxes with the right words.

1.

2.

3.

4.

5.

6.

B. One word is wrong in each sentence. Circle the wrong word. Then fill in the blank with a spelling word that makes sense.

1. I planted corn in the toaster, and it grew well. _____

2. My brother's little girl is my aunt. _____

3. The police chased the chair down the street. _____

4. Each person got a bucket of cake at the party. _____

5. The knights in the castle had a feather to protect them from flying arrows. _____

6. When you see the word "store," you must slow down and let others go first. _____

7. The head of a company is sometimes called its flower. _____

8. If you want people to listen to your speech, it should be boring and to the point. _____

C. Write the spelling words that end with a silent letter.

_____ _____

Name_____

Words with *ie*

thief	niece	field	brief
chief	piece	shield	yield

A. Use spelling words to complete the story.

My _____ and I were out for a ride in my car. Suddenly, I saw lights flash behind me. The _____ of police made us stop by the side of the road.

Did I run through a _____ sign, or did the chief think I was a _____? I was afraid I would get a ticket and have to pay a fine.

But the chief was very nice. He said a _____ of my taillight was broken. I thanked him and went on my way.

B. Write the spelling words in alphabetical order.

1. _____ 2. _____ 3. _____ 4. _____

5. _____ 6. _____ 7. _____ 8. _____

C. Use each spelling word in a sentence.

niece _____

field _____

brief _____

yield _____

shield _____

piece _____

chief _____

thief _____

Homonyms

road	pail	ate	see
rode	pale	eight	sea

A. Fill in each blank with a spelling word.

1. A _____ is a bucket in which you carry water.

2. _____ the horse running down the street!

3. You look as _____ as a ghost.

4. We stopped for a picnic on the side of the _____.

5. They _____ horses all day at the ranch.

6. We _____ too much watermelon at the party.

7. The huge aquarium had many _____ animals.

8. _____ people is too many to fit into a car.

B. Circle the right answers.

1. "Pail" and "pale" have different meanings, but they

    sound the same.   look the same.   feel the same.

2. The words in this lesson are called

    synonyms.   homonyms.   antonyms.

3. Words that sound the same but are not spelled the same are

    synonyms.   homonyms.   antonyms.

4. There are four sets of homonyms in this lesson.

    true   false

C. Find the missing letters. Then write the word.

1. p a ___ e   _____

2. e i ___ ___ ___   _____

Name _____

LESSON 9   Homonyms

road	pail	ate	see
rode	pale	eight	sea

A. Write the spelling words that rhyme with the words below.

1. showed   toad   _____

2. sail   tail   _____

3. date   bait   _____

4. be   fee   _____

5. fail   sail   _____

6. load   code   _____

7. rate   late   _____

B. Write a spelling word under each picture.

    8

1. _____   2. _____   3. _____

C. Write the spelling words in alphabetical order.

1. _____   2. _____   3. _____   4. _____

5. _____   6. _____   7. _____   8. _____

D. Write the words that name things you can touch.

1. _____   2. _____   3. _____

34

road	pail	ate	see
rode	pale	eight	sea

A. Use spelling words to complete the story.

My friends and I spent a week by the _____. We had a contest

to _____ who could build the best sand castle. We decided to start

at _____ o'clock in the morning.

On the day of the contest, I got up early. I _____ breakfast

and got a _____ to put the sand in. I _____ my bike down

to the shore.

We started building the castles. By ten o'clock, we were done. I had

worked hard on mine, and I was very tired. The sun was already turning

my face red.

I felt much better, though, when the winner was announced. My sand

castle won first prize.

B. Match each spelling word with the right clue.

_____	1. road	**a.**	the number after seven
_____	2. pail	**b.**	the ocean
_____	3. eight	**c.**	what you do with your eyes
_____	4. sea	**d.**	not having much color
_____	5. see	**e.**	a bucket for carrying water
_____	6. pale	**f.**	what cars travel on

Name _____

LESSON 9   Homonyms

road	pail	ate	see
rode	pale	eight	sea

A. Fill in the boxes with the right words.

1.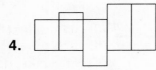

2.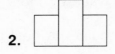

3.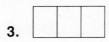

4.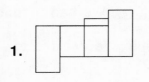

5.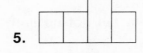

6.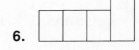

B. Use spelling words to complete the puzzle.

Across

2. the ocean

4. what your eyes do

6. I ___ a horse at the farm.

7. a bucket

Down

1. light in color

3. I ___ hot dogs for dinner last night.

5. comes after seven

6. a street

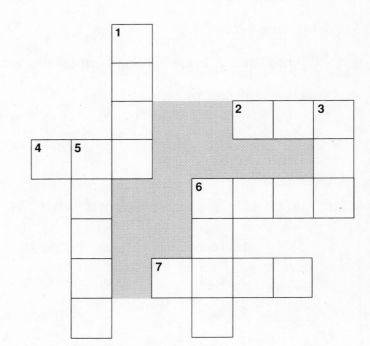

LESSON 10   Words with *ea*

breath	**thread**	**feather**	**weather**
spread	**ready**	**heavy**	**leather**

A. Fill in each blank with a spelling word.

1. Let's _____ out the food on the picnic table.

2. The chair was very _____.

3. A _____ fell off the duck's back.

4. Can you _____ the needle without your glasses?

5. Are you _____ to go to the store?

6. I was out of _____ at the end of the race.

7. The _____ will be hot and sunny today.

8. Do you wear a _____ belt?

B. Write a spelling word under each picture.

1. _____   2. _____   3. _____

C. Circle the letters that are the same in all the words.

breath   spread   thread   ready   feather   heavy   weather   leather

D. Write the words that name things you can touch.

1. _____   2. _____   3. _____

Name _____

Words with *ea*

breath	thread	feather	weather
spread	ready	heavy	leather

A. Fill in the boxes with the right words.

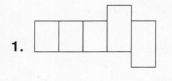
1.

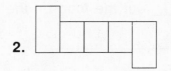
2.

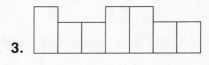
3.

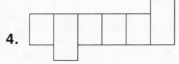
4.

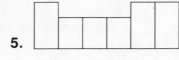
5.

6.

7.

8.

B. Match each spelling word with the right clue.

_____ 1. thread   **a.** what most shoes are made of

_____ 2. spread   **b.** can be rainy, sunny, cloudy, stormy, or cold

_____ 3. breath   **c.** how you put butter on bread

_____ 4. feather   **d.** what you use with a needle to sew clothes

_____ 5. weather   **e.** the air you breathe in or out

_____ 6. leather   **f.** one of what a chicken has instead of fur

C. Write the spelling words in alphabetical order.

1. _____   2. _____   3. _____

4. _____   5. _____   6. _____

7. _____   8. _____

Words with *ea*

breath	thread	feather	weather
spread	ready	heavy	leather

A. Find the hidden words on the list.

breath	ready	weather	trail
spread	feather	leather	plain
thread	heavy	mail	brain

```
j  a  s  o  n  i  f  e  a  t  h  e  r  s  l  m  y  s
s  o  n  h  r  y  a  n  s  f  r  i  t  e  e  n  d  p
t  h  e  e  y  p  b  r  a  i  n  l  r  a  a  y  t  r
o  g  e  a  t  h  e  r  i  n  t  h  a  e  t  s  w  e
t  i  m  v  m  i  b  r  e  a  t  h  i  g  h  p  o  a
h  o  l  y  t  h  e  y  l  i  k  e  l  t  e  o  l  d
r  i  s  t  e  n  t  o  s  t  o  r  i  e  r  s  t  h
e  a  p  l  a  i  n  w  e  a  t  h  e  r  t  j  a  s
a  o  n  s  m  o  m  t  a  m  m  y  r  e  a  d  s  t
d  o  t  h  e  m  a  i  l  m  s  h  r  e  a  d  y  e
```

B. Use spelling words to complete the story.

I helped my uncle make a cement porch. It wasn't as hard as I thought it would be. When the _____ was dry and sunny, we marked off the place the porch would go. Then we got the ground _____.

My uncle mixed the cement. Then we poured it in the place we had marked. After that, we had to work fast, before the cement got hard. We _____ it with a tool called a trowel. By the next day, the porch was dry. My uncle and I were proud of the porch we made.

© 1991 Steck-Vaughn Company. Target 780

Name _____

LESSON 10

Words with *ea*

breath	thread	feather	weather
spread	ready	heavy	leather

A. Find the missing letters. Then write the word.

1. s p ___ ___ ___ ___   _____

2. b r ___ ___ ___ h   _____

3. f ___ ___ t h ___ ___   _____

B. Use each spelling word in a sentence.

breath   _____

spread   _____

thread   _____

ready   _____

feather   _____

heavy   _____

weather   _____

leather   _____

C. One word is wrong in each sentence. Circle the wrong word. Then fill in the blank with a spelling word that makes sense.

1. The sofa is very green to pick up.   _____

2. I sewed it up with a needle and rope.   _____

3. She threw the jelly on the toast.   _____

4. We found a chicken tail in the soup.   _____

5. My belt is made of sand.   _____

40

Words with *ear*

| heard | earn | earth | hearse |
| learn | pearl | search | early |

A. Fill in each blank with a spelling word.

1. You have to get up _____ to get to school on time.

2. The diver found a _____ in the oyster.

3. Dirt is also called _____.

4. A _____ is a car at a funeral home.

5. We had to _____ for our lost kitten.

6. How much money do you _____ on your paper route?

7. I _____ that story when I was a child.

8. What did you _____ in school today?

B. Circle the letters that are the same in all the words.

heard   learn   earn   pearl   earth   search   hearse   early

C. Write the spelling words that rhyme with the words below.

1. bird   third   _____

2. curl   girl   _____

3. church   perch   _____

4. burn   fern   _____

5. verse   curse   _____

6. curly   surly   _____

7. birth   worth   _____

Name _____

LESSON 11

Words with *ear*

heard	earn	earth	hearse
learn	pearl	search	early

A. Put an *X* on the word that is <u>not</u> the same.

1. heard	heard	hard	heard	heard
2. learn	lean	learn	learn	learn
3. earn	earn	earn	earn	earn
4. pearl	qearl	pearl	pearl	pearl
5. earth	earth	earht	earth	earth
6. search	sarch	search	search	search
7. hearse	hearse	harse	hearse	hearse

B. Write a spelling word under each picture.

1. _____   2. _____   3. _____

C. Write the words that name things you cannot touch.

1. _____   2. _____   3. _____

4. _____   5. _____

D. Write the spelling words in alphabetical order.

1. _____   2. _____   3. _____   4. _____

5. _____   6. _____   7. _____   8. _____

42

Words with *ear*

heard	earn	earth	hearse
learn	pearl	search	early

A. Use spelling words to complete the story.

Have you _____ how an oyster makes a _____?

It starts with an accident _____ in an oyster's life. A bit of sand gets in the oyster's shell. The lining of the shell starts to cover the piece of sand. Layers of the shell lining build up over the years. Finally, a pearl is formed.

You have to look in many oysters to find just one pearl. But the _____ is worth it. A perfect, round pearl is worth a lot of money.

People have studied oysters to _____ how to get them to make pearls. A piece of sand or shell can be put into young oysters. Then the oysters are kept in special cages. After a few years, about one out of twenty oysters will have a beautiful pearl inside its shell.

B. Fill in the boxes with the right words.

1.

2.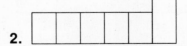

3.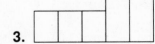

4. (boxes)

5.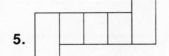

6.

7.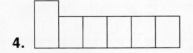

8. (boxes)

Name _____

Words with *ear*

heard	earn	earth	hearse
learn	pearl	search	early

A. **Find the missing letters. Then write the word.**

1. ___ e a r ___ e   _____

2. ___ ___ ___ t h   _____

B. **Match each spelling word with the right clue.**

_____ **1.** pearl

_____ **2.** search

_____ **3.** earn

_____ **4.** hearse

_____ **5.** earth

_____ **6.** learn

a. to get to know something by study or practice

b. to deserve or win

c. a white jewel formed in oysters

d. a car that takes the dead to be buried

e. to look for something

f. dirt or soil

C. **Use each spelling word in a sentence.**

heard _____

learn _____

earn _____

pearl _____

earth _____

search _____

hearse _____

early _____

Words with -*y*

cry	dry	fly	spy
fry	shy	sky	pry

A. Fill in each blank with a spelling word.

1. The _____ is very blue today.

2. Do you _____ your clothes on the line outside?

3. Let's _____ the fish over the campfire.

4. I began to _____ when I heard the bad news.

5. The puppy was so _____ that it hid inside the box.

6. I'm going to swat that _____!

7. She had to _____ the lid off the jar.

8. You should not _____ on your friends.

B. Complete these exercises with spelling words.

1. Which words end with *ry*?

   _____   _____   _____   _____

2. Which words begin with *s*?

   _____   _____   _____

3. Which words do these words come from?

   pries _____   spies _____

   dries _____   cries _____

   fries _____   flies _____

C. Circle the letter that is the same in all the words.

cry   fry   dry   shy   fly   sky   spy   pry

Name _____

Words with -y

cry	dry	fly	spy
fry	shy	sky	pry

A. Put an *X* on the word that is <u>not</u> the same.

1. cry	cry	cny	cry	cry
2. fry	fny	fry	fry	fry
3. dry	dry	dry	dry	bry
4. shy	shy	sby	shy	shy
5. fly	flg	fly	fly	fly

B. Fill in the boxes with the right words.

1.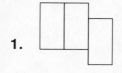

2.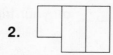

3.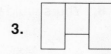

4.

5.

6.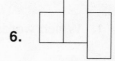

C. Use each spelling word in a sentence.

cry _____

fry _____

dry _____

shy _____

fly _____

sky _____

spy _____

pry _____

Words with -*y*

cry	dry	fly	spy
fry	shy	sky	pry

A. Use spelling words to complete the story.

I love good _____ movies. They keep you on the edge of

your seat.

My favorite actor played a spy named James Bond. He had special

cars that could do everything but _____. Even his watch was full

of tricks.

In one movie, a mean man puts a deadly spider in James Bond's bed.

You see the spider crawl across Bond's chest. Whenever I see this part, I

_____ out, "Don't move!" But things always turn out all right for him.

I'd love to meet this actor in person. But I'm sure I'd be too

_____ to even speak to him.

B. Write the spelling words in alphabetical order.

1. _____   2. _____   3. _____   4. _____

5. _____   6. _____   7. _____   8. _____

C. Finish the sentences. Use a dictionary if you need to.

1. "Cry" means _____.

2. "Spy" means _____.

3. "Shy" means _____.

4. "Pry" means _____.

Name _____

Words with -y

cry	dry	fly	spy
fry	shy	sky	pry

A. Match each spelling word with its opposite word.

_____ **1.** cry   **a.** ground

_____ **2.** dry   **b.** outgoing

_____ **3.** sky   **c.** laugh

_____ **4.** shy   **d.** wet

B. Add *ing* to the spelling words below. Then write sentences using the new words.

cry   *crying   The baby is crying.* _____

dry   _____   _____

fly   _____   _____

spy   _____   _____

fry   _____   _____

pry   _____   _____

C. Complete these exercises with spelling words.

1. Write the word that has to do with cooking.

_____

2. Write the word that tells what birds do.

_____

3. Write the word that tells where clouds float.

_____

Homonyms

to	for	bear	flour
two	four	bare	flower

A. Fill in each blank with a spelling word.

1. She ran out of the house in her _____ feet.

2. This cake calls for sifted _____.

3. Please open the door _____ me.

4. Half of a month is about _____ weeks.

5. Will you go with me _____ the party?

6. Two, _____ six, eight! Who do we appreciate?

7. Did you see that big _____ in the park?

8. They gave their mother a pretty _____ for her birthday.

B. Complete these exercises with spelling words.

1. Write the words that have both *a* and *e* in them.

   _____   _____

2. Write the shortest word. _____

3. Write the longest word. _____

4. Write the words that are numbers.

   _____   _____

C. Write a spelling word under each picture.

      4

1. _____   2. _____   3. _____

Name _____

Homonyms

to	for	bear	flour
two	four	bare	flower

A. Fill in the boxes with the right words.

1.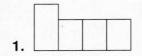

2.

3.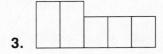

4.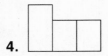

5.

6.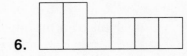

B. Circle the right answers.

1. The four sets of words in this lesson are

synonyms.   homonyms.   antonyms.

2. One word has as many letters as the number it is.

for   four

3. One of the *b* words is an animal. It is

bear.   bare.

4. One of the words is visited by bees. It is

flour.   flower.

5. Two of the words are living things.

true   false

C. Write the spelling words in alphabetical order.

1. _____   2. _____   3. _____   4. _____

5. _____   6. _____   7. _____   8. _____

Homonyms

to	for	bear	flour
two	four	bare	flower

A. Find the hidden words on the list.

to	four	flour	coast
two	bear	flower	load
for	bare	toast	road

```
p  o  d  f  b  o  u  r  r  h  f  a  s  f  o  u  r
j  u  d  y  a  a  n  d  o  d  l  o  a  d  e  n  i
s  e  a  n  r  d  b  a  a  r  o  b  a  r  a  a  n
d  b  t  r  e  b  a  r  d  a  u  a  n  c  d  a  t
f  l  s  o  p  f  h  e  r  n  r  e  s  o  h  e  w
o  y  h  a  v  l  e  f  i  f  t  h  a  a  d  d  o
r  s  i  x  t  o  a  s  t  t  h  g  r  s  a  d  e
r  s  a  n  d  w  i  l  i  k  e  t  h  t  e  m  a
l  l  v  e  r  e  y  m  u  c  h  t  h  e  y  d  o
l  o  t  s  o  r  f  t  h  g  o  o  b  e  a  r  d
```

B. Match each spelling word with the right clue.

_____	1. bear	**a.**	this is used to make bread
_____	2. flower	**b.**	the opposite of "from"
_____	3. flour	**c.**	an animal with thick fur, short legs, and dangerous claws
_____	4. two	**d.**	the number after three
_____	5. to	**e.**	without covering or clothing
_____	6. four	**f.**	the number after one
_____	7. bare	**g.**	the blossom of a plant

Name _____

LESSON 13 — Homonyms

to	for	bear	flour
two	four	bare	flower

A. Use spelling words to complete the story.

We were on a campout. It was my turn _____ go into town for

food. The store was just _____ miles from camp, so I went on foot.

On the way, I stopped to admire a _____. Right beside the

flowers were some paw prints. I bent down and studied the prints. I'd seen

them before in a book.

They looked like _____ tracks. Bears! I ran _____ my

life back to camp.

B. Use each spelling word in a sentence.

to _____

two _____

for _____

four _____

bear _____

bare _____

flour _____

flower _____

C. Find the missing letters. Then write the word.

1. f ___ ___ ___ e r   _____

2. b ___ ___ r   _____

Words with *eigh*

sleigh	weigh	neighbor	eighty
freight	weight	neigh	freighter

A. Fill in each blank with a spelling word.

1. A _____ is a ship that carries cargo.

2. Let's go on a _____ ride in the snow.

3. The doctor will _____ you on the scale.

4. The _____ on the truck was fruits and vegetables.

5. The hog's _____ was 300 pounds.

6. My _____ next door has a very nice yard.

7. The horse gave a loud _____ and threw off its rider.

8. There were _____ people on the jet plane.

B. Circle the letters that are the same in all the words.

sleigh   freight   weigh   weight   neighbor   neigh   eighty   freighter

C. Write the spelling words that rhyme with the words below.

1. day   ray   _____

2. date   rate   _____

D. One word is wrong in each sentence. Circle the wrong word. Then fill in the blank with a spelling word that makes sense.

1. She is my next-door tractor.   _____

2. Should you diet to lose some height?   _____

3. It's fun to ride a snake in the snow.   _____

Name _____

Words with *eigh*

sleigh	weigh	neighbor	eighty
freight	weight	neigh	freighter

A. Find the hidden words on the list.

sleigh	weight	eighty	shade
freight	neighbor	freighter	flake
weigh	neigh	blade	snake

```
s  s  o  t  o  d  a  s  l  e  i  g  h  y  i  s  n
h  f  r  e  i  g  h  t  e  r  e  n  f  a  b  n  e
a  d  i  f  a  m  w  e  i  g  h  w  l  o  l  r  i
d  k  i  r  n  g  h  a  r  d  o  n  a  t  a  h  g
e  i  s  e  a  g  w  e  i  g  h  t  k  a  d  i  h
n  s  o  i  o  n  i  l  w  i  l  l  e  b  e  e  b
b  a  c  g  k  a  t  g  s  e  a  w  e  l  l  w  o
i  t  h  h  v  a  l  h  e  r  s  n  a  k  e  i  r
a  a  n  t  d  o  r  t  b  a  r  b  a  r  a  l  a
n  e  i  g  h  w  l  e  r  a  n  e  i  g  h  t  y
```

B. Write a spelling word under each picture.

80

1. _____   2. _____   3. _____

C. Write the spelling words in alphabetical order.

1. _____   2. _____   3. _____   4. _____

5. _____   6. _____   7. _____   8. _____

Words with *eigh*

sleigh	weigh	neighbor	eighty
freight	weight	neigh	freighter

A. Use spelling words to complete the story.

I had a _____ once who was almost _____ years old. He liked to tell me stories. When he was a young man, he used to work on a _____. A freighter is a ship that carries freight. His job was to _____ the freight as it was loaded on the ship. Sometimes the freight would weigh a lot. Then he would have to figure out how much to charge the owners.

B. Match each spelling word with the right clue.

_____ 1. neighbor   **a.** goods that are carried by land, sea, or air

_____ 2. sleigh   **b.** someone who lives close to you

_____ 3. freight   **c.** the amount that something weighs

_____ 4. weigh   **d.** the sound a horse makes

_____ 5. neigh   **e.** a ship carrying cargo

_____ 6. weight   **f.** what you do to find the weight of something

_____ 7. eighty   **g.** a vehicle to ride in through the snow

_____ 8. freighter   **h.** the number after 79

C. Write the words that name things you can touch.

1. _____   2. _____   3. _____

4. _____

Name _____

Words with *eigh*

sleigh	weigh	neighbor	eighty
freight	weight	neigh	freighter

A. Put an *X* on the word that is <u>not</u> the same.

1. sleigh	sleigh	sleihg	sleigh	sleigh
2. freight	freight	freight	freighf	freight
3. weigh	wiegh	weigh	weigh	weigh
4. weight	weight	weight	weight	weighf
5. neighbor	neighbor	neighdor	neighbor	neighbor
6. neigh	neigh	neijh	neigh	neigh
7. eighty	eihgty	eighty	eighty	eighty

B. Circle the right answers.

1. Seventy-nine is close to this.

      eight   eighty

2. Most trucks on the road carry this.

      sleigh   freight   neighbor

3. This is a person.

      freight   neighbor   sleigh

4. This is something that you ride in.

      neigh   sleigh   weigh

5. You find this out when you read scales.

      weight   freight   eight

6. This is something we all have.

      freight   sleigh   weight

Words with *kn-*

kneel	knife	knot	knight
knock	knit	knob	knack

A. Fill in each blank with a spelling word.

1. The door _____ fell off when I touched it.

2. Did you _____ that pretty sweater?

3. Scouts learn how to tie a _____ with a rope.

4. She has a _____ for saying the right thing.

5. A _____ was a soldier in King Arthur's court.

6. I cut my finger on a sharp _____.

7. Please _____ before you come in my room.

8. You have to _____ down to work in the garden.

B. Circle the letters that are the same in all the words.

kneel   knock   knife   knit   knot   knob   knight   knack

C. Write the spelling words that rhyme with the words below.

1. sock   rock   _____

2. fit   kit   _____

3. bite   kite   _____

4. cot   lot   _____

5. wife   life   _____

6. feel   peel   _____

7. cob   sob   _____

8. sack   pack   _____

Name _____

LESSON 15

Words with *kn-*

kneel	**knife**	**knot**	**knight**
knock	**knit**	**knob**	**knack**

A. Put an *X* on the word that is <u>not</u> the same.

1. kneel	knell	kneel	kneel	kneel
2. knock	knock	knock	knock	kneck
3. knife	knife	knite	knife	knife
4. knit	knit	knit	kmit	knit
5. knot	knof	knot	knot	knot
6. knob	knod	knob	knob	knob
7. knight	knight	knighf	knight	knight
8. knack	knack	knack	kacnk	knack

B. Match each spelling word with the right clue.

_____ 1. knack   **a.** a kitchen tool used for cutting

_____ 2. knight   **b.** a round handle for opening a door

_____ 3. knob   **c.** a talent for doing something

_____ 4. knot   **d.** a soldier who fights for a king or queen

_____ 5. knit   **e.** a fastening or a tangle

_____ 6. knife   **f.** to hit or rap

_____ 7. knock   **g.** to go down on your knees

_____ 8. kneel   **h.** to loop yarn together for clothes

C. Write the words that name things you can touch.

1. _____ 2. _____ 3. _____ 4. _____

LESSON 15

Words with *kn-*

kneel	knife	knot	knight
knock	knit	knob	knack

A. Use spelling words to complete the story.

In the woods lived a man with a _____ for solving problems.

One day there was a _____ at the man's door. The king had come

to ask the man to help his daughter, the princess. Someone had put a spell

on the princess and turned her into a mouse.

The man went back to the castle with the king. He asked to see the

mouse. Then he pulled a _____ out of his pocket. He cut off a bit

of the mouse's hair. He spoke some words of magic. The mouse turned

back into the princess.

The king was very happy. He had the man _____ before him

and made him a _____ of the royal court.

B. Write a spelling word under each picture.

1. _____   2. _____   3. _____

C. Fill in the boxes with the right words.

1. 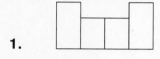   2. 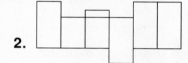   3.

4.   5.   6.

Words with *kn-*

kneel	knife	knot	knight
knock	knit	knob	knack

A. Find the missing letters. Then write the word.

1. k ___ ___ ___ ___ t   _____

2. k ___ ___ ___ e   _____

B. Match each spelling word with a related word.

_____ **1.** kneel   **a.** fork

_____ **2.** knock   **b.** door

_____ **3.** knife   **c.** talent

_____ **4.** knit   **d.** rap

_____ **5.** knot   **e.** soldier

_____ **6.** knob   **f.** sweater

_____ **7.** knight   **g.** rope

_____ **8.** knack   **h.** bend

C. Complete these exercises with spelling words.

1. Which words end with *ck*?

_____   _____

2. Which words have the long *i* sound?

_____   _____

3. Which words have the short *o* sound?

_____   _____   _____

4. Which word has the long *e* sound?   _____

Words with *wr-*

wrench	wrist	wreck	wren
wring	wrong	wrestle	wreath

A. Fill in each blank with a spelling word.

1. She was in a very bad car _____.

2. Do you like the Christmas _____ on our door?

3. The bird singing outside is a _____.

4. The police had to _____ the man to the ground.

5. He began to _____ his hands when he got upset.

6. It is _____ to cheat on a test.

7. He broke his _____ in the football game.

8. I need a _____ to fix the sink.

B. Write the spelling words that rhyme with the words below.

1. sing   bring   _____

2. fist   list   _____

3. song   long   _____

4. deck   neck   _____

5. pen   ten   _____

6. teeth   sheath   _____

C. Write a spelling word under each picture.

1. _____   2. _____   3. _____

Name_____

Words with *wr-*

wrench	wrist	wreck	wren
wring	wrong	wrestle	wreath

A. Circle the letters that are the same in all the words.

wrench   wring   wrist   wrong   wreck   wrestle   wren   wreath

B. Which letter is silent in all the spelling words? _____

C. Use spelling words to complete the puzzle.

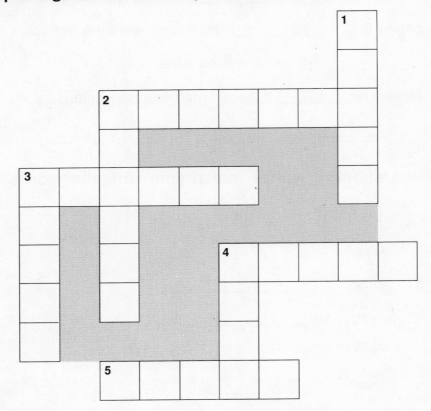

Across

2. to fight hand to hand

3. a tool

4. between the hand and arm

5. to squeeze out or twist

Down

1. Two cars had a ___.

2. a ring of leaves

3. incorrect

4. a songbird

Words with *wr-*

wrench	wrist	wreck	wren
wring	wrong	wrestle	wreath

A. Use spelling words to complete the story.

My friend and I were riding in her car, when we saw a line of cars ahead. We knew something was _____. All the cars in our lane began to slow down. Two cars had run into each other. One of the drivers who was in the _____ sat on the curb holding his _____.

The police were there. They had to use a _____ to pry open the other driver's door. Both drivers looked frightened, but no one was badly hurt.

B. Match each spelling word with a related word.

_____ **1.** wreath   **a.** crash

_____ **2.** wren   **b.** watch

_____ **3.** wrestle   **c.** incorrect

_____ **4.** wreck   **d.** bird

_____ **5.** wrong   **e.** decoration

_____ **6.** wrist   **f.** fight

_____ **7.** wring   **g.** tool

_____ **8.** wrench   **h.** twist

C. Write the words that name things you can touch.

1. _____ 2. _____ 3. _____

4. _____ 5. _____

Name _____

Words with *wr-*

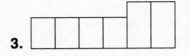
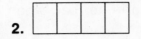
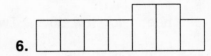

| wrench | wrist | wreck | wren |
| wring | wrong | wrestle | wreath |

A. Fill in the boxes with the right words.

1.

2.

3.

4.

5.

6.

B. Write the spelling words in alphabetical order.

1. _____ 2. _____ 3. _____ 4. _____

5. _____ 6. _____ 7. _____ 8. _____

C. Use each spelling word in a sentence.

wrench _____

wring _____

wrist _____

wrong _____

wreck _____

wrestle _____

wren _____

wreath _____

D. Find the missing letters. Then write the word.

1. ____ r ____ ____   _____

2. w r ____ ____ t   _____

64

won't	isn't	didn't	hasn't
aren't	doesn't	wasn't	weren't

A. Fill in each blank with a spelling word.

1. We _____ ready to go yet.

2. One twin does well in art, but the other twin _____.

3. I _____ feeling well last week.

4. He _____ be able to go with us.

5. He _____ had his dinner yet.

6. _____ you the captain of the team last time?

7. Earth _____ the largest planet.

8. We almost won today, _____ we?

B. Circle the letters that are the same in all the words.

won't   aren't   isn't   doesn't   didn't   wasn't   hasn't   weren't

C. Complete these exercises.

1. What word does *n't* stand for? _____

2. The words in this lesson are called

    homonyms.   contractions.   compounds.

D. Find the missing letters. Then write the word.

1. ___ r e ___ ' ___   _____

2. h ___ s n ' ___   _____

3. d ___ ___ ___ n ' t   _____

Name _____

Contractions with *-n't*

won't	isn't	didn't	hasn't
aren't	doesn't	wasn't	weren't

A. The spelling words are called contractions. Match the two words to the contraction.

_____ **1.** isn't   **a.** were not

_____ **2.** doesn't   **b.** are not

_____ **3.** hasn't   **c.** will not

_____ **4.** weren't   **d.** did not

_____ **5.** won't   **e.** is not

_____ **6.** aren't   **f.** does not

_____ **7.** didn't   **g.** has not

B. Put an *X* on the word that is <u>not</u> the same.

1. aren't	aren't	aren't	aren't	aern't
2. didn't	didn't	dibn't	didn't	didn't
3. won't	wou't	won't	won't	won't

C. Use spelling words to complete the puzzle.

Across

3. is not

4. were not

5. has not

Down

1. did not

2. are not

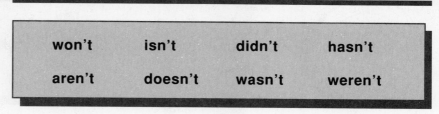

Contractions with -n't

won't	isn't	didn't	hasn't
aren't	doesn't	wasn't	weren't

A. Find the hidden words on the list. The words are written without an (').

won't	doesn't	hasn't	state
aren't	didn't	weren't	tame
isn't	wasn't	plate	flame

```
h  s  y  h  e  r  w  a  s  n  t  d  d  n  l  b  h
o  f  a  o  d  o  n  t  t  d  a  h  i  g  i  u  a
m  l  t  o  o  p  i  e  l  i  w  e  d  a  p  t  s
a  a  a  r  e  n  t  r  e  s  h  l  n  n  l  m  n
s  m  o  l  s  e  r  m  f  n  o  p  t  d  a  o  t
w  e  u  s  n  p  e  y  r  t  n  i  a  s  t  s  a
o  v  r  o  t  p  m  w  e  r  e  n  t  p  e  t  l
r  e  s  d  s  e  e  l  i  l  e  n  d  e  n  o  l
s  t  a  t  e  r  m  i  e  w  o  n  t  a  m  e  i
```

B. Write the spelling words in alphabetical order.

1. _____ 2. _____ 3. _____ 4. _____

5. _____ 6. _____ 7. _____ 8. _____

C. Circle the word that is the same as the top one.

won't	aren't	isn't	doesn't	didn't	wasn't	hasn't	weren't
bon't	aren't	isn'f	boesn't	dibn't	wasn't	basn't	waren't
won't	arem't	sin't	dosen't	didn't	wasm't	hasm't	weren't
dom't	anen't	isn't	daesn't	didn'f	wasn'f	hasn't	werem't
don'f	aren'f	ism't	doesn't	didm't	wosn't	hosn't	weren'f

Name _____

Contractions with -n't

won't	isn't	didn't	hasn't
aren't	doesn't	wasn't	weren't

A. Fill in each blank with the right word.

1. She _____ have any money.
   isn't   doesn't

2. They _____ going to the zoo today.
   weren't   wasn't

3. He _____ the one who has the ball.
   aren't   isn't

4. It _____ been long since they left.
   weren't   hasn't

5. She _____ know how to work the math problem.
   didn't   hasn't

6. It _____ their fault that they were late.
   wasn't   weren't

7. They _____ have any more to eat.
   doesn't   won't

8. _____ you tired of all the noise?
   Isn't   Aren't

B. Use spelling words to complete the story.

My little brother is six years old. He likes to play baseball. He

_____ a very good player yet, but that _____ bother him.

He knows he'll get better with practice.

He is good at throwing the ball. But he _____ run to catch the

ball if it's far away. He also needs to practice batting. He struck out three

times in the last game he played.

I'm going to help him become a better player.

LESSON 18   Homonyms

blew	hear	sale	knew
blue	here	sail	new

A. Fill in each blank with a spelling word.

1. The store is having a _____ on clothes.

2. The truck _____ a tire and ran off the road.

3. He is _____ today to talk to you.

4. I _____ her when she was just a little girl.

5. Did you _____ what he said?

6. The sky is so clear and _____ today.

7. They will _____ around the world on a ship.

8. Are you a _____ student, or were you here last year?

B. Circle the right answers.

1. The words in today's lessons are

    synonyms.   homonyms.   antonyms.

2. "Blue" and "blew" are not spelled alike, but they

    sound alike.   feel alike.   mean the same thing.

3. The word that begins with a silent letter is

    sail.   blew.   here.   knew.

C. Write the spelling words that rhyme with the words below.

1. do   flew   _____

2. ear   dear   _____

3. jail   fail   _____

Name _____   69

LESSON 18 — Homonyms

blew	hear	sale	knew
blue	here	sail	new

A. Fill in the boxes with the right words.

1.

2.

3.

4.

5.

6.

7.

8.

B. Match each spelling word with the right clue.

_____	**1.** knew	**a.**	the act of selling
_____	**2.** sale	**b.**	a "sheet" for catching wind on a ship
_____	**3.** hear	**c.**	the opposite of "old"
_____	**4.** blew	**d.**	where you are right now
_____	**5.** new	**e.**	a color
_____	**6.** sail	**f.**	what the wind did yesterday
_____	**7.** here	**g.**	what you do with your ears
_____	**8.** blue	**h.**	used to know

C. Write the spelling words in alphabetical order.

1. _____ 2. _____ 3. _____ 4. _____

5. _____ 6. _____ 7. _____ 8. _____

70

Homonyms

blew	hear	sale	knew
blue	here	sail	new

A. Use spelling words to complete the story.

When I was ten years old we moved _____ to be near the

ocean. This was a _____ kind of life for us at first, but we quickly

got used to it. I love the water and sun and sand. You can wear shorts here

all the time.

The family next door became our best friends. My mother says she

_____ right away we'd get along. She was right. We enjoy the same

things. We like to spend time on the beach. In summer we _____

our boats together in the bay. On weekends we fish from the pier and cook

our catch outdoors.

We're lucky to live by the ocean. We can go to the beach every day.

B. Put an X on the word that is not the same.

1. hear	hare	hear	hear	hear
2. sale	sale	sale	sael	sale
3. knew	knew	knew	knew	know
4. new	now	new	new	new
5. blew	blew	blew	blow	blew
6. blue	blue	bule	blue	blue
7. here	here	here	heer	here
8. sail	sali	sail	sail	sail

Homonyms

blew	hear	sale	knew
blue	here	sail	new

A. **Find the missing letters. Then write the word.**

1. b ____ ____ e   _____

2. ____ ____ l ____   _____

B. **Complete these exercises with spelling words.**

1. Which words end with *ew*?

_____   _____   _____

2. Which word does not have the letter *e* in it? _____

C. **Use each spelling word in a sentence.**

blew _____

blue _____

hear _____

here _____

sale _____

sail _____

knew _____

new _____

D. **Write the words that name things you cannot touch.**

1. _____ 2. _____ 3. _____

4. _____ 5. _____ 6. _____

Contractions with -'ll and -'ve

I'll	she'll	I've	we've
you'll	he'll	you've	they've

A. Fill in each blank with a spelling word.

1. My sister says _____ go to summer school.

2. If you tell me a secret, _____ never repeat it.

3. _____ got a quarter in my pocket.

4. You must be careful, or _____ hurt yourself.

5. _____ won all their games this year.

6. If _____ never been to the sea, you should go.

7. If a peacock wants to show off, _____ spread his tail feathers.

8. _____ got five people in our family.

B. Circle the letters that are the same in all the words.

I've   you've   we've   they've

C. Answer the questions.

1. What word does 've stand for? _____

2. What word does 'll stand for? _____

D. Find the missing letters. Then write the word.

1. ___ ___ e ' l l   _____

2. ___ ___ ___ ___ ' v e   _____

3. y ___ ___ ' ___ l   _____

© 1991 Steck-Vaughn Company. Target 780

Name _____

Contractions with *-'ll* and *-'ve*

I'll	she'll	I've	we've
you'll	he'll	you've	they've

A. Match the two words to the contraction.

_____ **1.** she'll

_____ **2.** he'll

_____ **3.** you'll

_____ **4.** I'll

_____ **5.** we've

_____ **6.** they've

_____ **7.** I've

a. they have

b. you will

c. we have

d. I have

e. she will

f. he will

g. I will

B. Fill in the boxes with the right words.

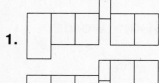      

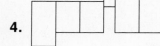   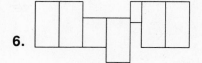

C. Use spelling words to complete the puzzle.

Across

1. they have

4. I have

5. she will

Down

2. you have

3. we have

4. I will

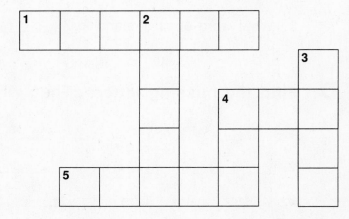

Contractions with -'ll and -'ve

I'll	she'll	I've	we've
you'll	he'll	you've	they've

A. Find the hidden words on the list. The words are written without an (').

life	they've	she'll	wife	we've
you've	strike	you'll	bike	

```
s  o  m  e  w  h  e  r  e  o  v  e  r  t  h  y  e
r  w  e  l  l  a  l  i  f  e  i  n  b  o  w  o  w
a  y  u  p  h  i  g  h  t  h  e  r  e  s  a  u  l
a  s  n  d  y  t  h  a  t  i  h  l  e  t  a  v  w
r  h  d  o  o  f  w  i  f  e  o  l  n  h  c  e  e
i  e  n  a  u  l  u  l  k  a  b  l  y  e  s  o  v
m  l  e  l  l  w  h  e  r  e  o  v  e  y  r  t  e
h  l  e  v  l  r  b  i  k  e  a  i  n  v  b  o  w
s  k  i  e  s  a  r  e  b  l  u  e  a  e  n  d  t
h  e  d  r  e  a  s  t  r  i  k  e  m  s  t  h  a
```

B. Use spelling words to complete the story.

Some of us were talking about where _____ been on trips. I told the group that _____ never been out of the state. Others said _____ only seen one other state.

"That's hard to believe," said a man. "You mean _____ never been out West or seen the Rocky Mountains?"

"No," I told him. "There's so much to see in my own state, I haven't had time to see anything else."

Name _____

Contractions with -'ll and -'ve

I'll	she'll	I've	we've
you'll	he'll	you've	they've

A. Fill in each blank with the right word.

1. _____ be at school on time, won't you?
   You've   You'll

2. _____ never been there before.
   I'll   I've

3. _____ see you in town on Friday.
   She'll   We've

4. I know _____ be glad to see you.
   you've   he'll

5. _____ look both ways before I cross the street again.
   You've   I'll

6. _____ always looked after each other.
   They've   You'll

7. _____ always tried to do our best work.
   We've   You'll

8. _____ been a joy to teach this year.
   He'll   You've

B. Finish the sentences.

1. I've never thought _____.

2. We've always wished _____.

C. Write the spelling words in alphabetical order.

1. _____ 2. _____ 3. _____ 4. _____

5. _____ 6. _____ 7. _____ 8. _____

76

Words with *-shes*

| bushes | crushes | brushes | washes |
| wishes | flashes | dishes | fishes |

A. Fill in each blank with a spelling word.

1. The camera _____ in my face.

2. She _____ her hair before she goes to bed.

3. The cat _____ its paws until they are clean.

4. We planted lots of _____ in our yard.

5. The sign at the magic well said, "You may have three _____."

6. The blender _____ ice very well.

7. Is it your turn to do the _____?

8. My uncle _____ in the pond on his farm.

B. Circle the letters that are the same in all the words.

bushes   wishes   crushes   flashes   brushes   dishes   washes   fishes

C. Write a spelling word under each picture.

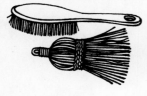   

1. _____ 2. _____ 3. _____ 4. _____

D. Write the spelling words in alphabetical order.

1. _____ 2. _____ 3. _____ 4. _____

5. _____ 6. _____ 7. _____ 8. _____

Name _____

Words with *-shes*

bushes	crushes	brushes	washes
wishes	flashes	dishes	fishes

A. Put an X on the word that is not the same.

1. bushes	dushes	bushes	bushes	bushes
2. wishes	wishes	wishes	mishes	wishes
3. crushes	crushes	cnushes	crushes	crushes
4. flashes	flashes	flashes	flashes	flaches
5. brushes	brushes	drushes	brushes	brushes
6. dishes	dishes	bishes	dishes	dishes
7. washes	mashes	washes	washes	washes
8. fishes	tishes	fishes	fishes	fishes

B. Match each spelling word with the right clue.

_____ 1. fishes	**a.** what a garbage truck does to trash
_____ 2. washes	**b.** plates, bowls, and cups
_____ 3. brushes	**c.** what the bulb on a camera does
_____ 4. dishes	**d.** hopeful dreams
_____ 5. crushes	**e.** more than one brush
_____ 6. flashes	**f.** what a washer does
_____ 7. wishes	**g.** what one does with a rod and reel
_____ 8. bushes	**h.** shrubs or large woody plants

C. Write the words that name things you can touch.

1. _____ 2. _____ 3. _____ 4. _____

Words with -shes

bushes	crushes	brushes	washes
wishes	flashes	dishes	fishes

A. Use spelling words to complete the story.

I know a man who loves to cook, so he opened a small cafe. The cafe is a few miles out of town. He serves very good food there. But it keeps him busy all the time.

On his day off, he _____ for trout to serve at the cafe. He cleans the fish himself. His wife makes the breads and desserts. She also helps seat the guests. His son helps wash the _____. The oldest daughter _____ and irons the napkins and tablecloths. Sometimes she serves the food. Much of what they cook is grown in their own garden.

The man says he _____ he had more free time. "But if I did," he says, "I'd probably just spend it cooking."

B. Write the simplest form of each spelling word.

1. _____ 2. _____ 3. _____ 4. _____

5. _____ 6. _____ 7. _____ 8. _____

C. Fill in the boxes with the right words.

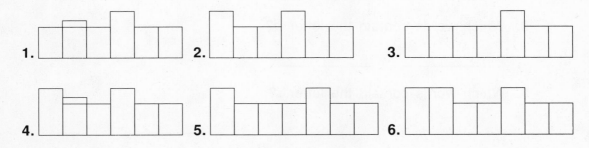

1.

2.

3.

4.

5.

6.

Name _____

Words with *-shes*

bushes	crushes	brushes	washes
wishes	flashes	dishes	fishes

A. Find the missing letters. Then write the word.

1. b r __ __ __ __ __   _____

2. __ l __ __ __ __ __   _____

3. w i __ __ __ __   _____

B. Use each spelling word in a sentence.

bushes _____

wishes _____

crushes _____

flashes _____

brushes _____

dishes _____

washes _____

fishes _____

C. Complete these exercises with spelling words.

1. Which words begin with two consonants?

   _____   _____   _____

2. Which words contain the letter *a*?

   _____   _____

3. Which words contain the letter *i*?

   _____   _____   _____

boxes	fixes	taxes	mixes
foxes	waxes	axes	sixes

A. Fill in each blank with a spelling word.

1. The helper _____ the floor to make it shine.

2. We pay _____ each year to help support our government.

3. There are many cake _____ to choose from.

4. Six _____ is thirty-six.

5. We piled the _____ on top of each other.

6. A plumber _____ stopped-up sinks.

7. Lumberjacks use _____ to cut down trees.

8. The farmer put up a fence to keep out _____.

B. Circle the letters that are the same in all the words.

boxes   foxes   fixes   waxes   taxes   axes   mixes   sixes

C. Write the spelling words in alphabetical order.

1. _____   2. _____   3. _____   4. _____

5. _____   6. _____   7. _____   8. _____

D. Write the words that name things you can touch.

1. _____   2. _____   3. _____

4. _____   5. _____

© 1991 Steck-Vaughn Company. Target 780

Name _____

Words with *-xes*

boxes	fixes	taxes	mixes
foxes	waxes	axes	sixes

A. Write the simplest form of each spelling word.

1. _____ 2. _____ 3. _____ 4. _____

5. _____ 6. _____ 7. _____ 8. _____

B. Use spelling words to complete the story.

I like to go to the dock to watch the ships unload. They bring goods from all parts of the world.

The goods come in _____. They're unpacked and sold here. But before the boxes can be unloaded, _____ must be paid on them.

The boxes all have numbers so that no one _____ them up. I like to imagine what's in the boxes.

C. Write a spelling word under each picture.

   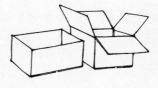

1. _____ 2. _____ 3. _____ 4. _____

D. Find the missing letters. Then write the word.

1. f o __ __ __   _____

2. a __ __ __   _____

Words with -xes

boxes	fixes	taxes	mixes
foxes	waxes	axes	sixes

A. Find the hidden words on the list.

boxes	waxes	mixes	spine
foxes	taxes	sixes	ripe
fixes	axes	vine	stripe

```
j  a  c  k  a  s  p  i  n  e  n  d  j  r  i  p  e
m  i  l  l  w  e  n  t  u  p  t  h  w  e  h  i  l
i  l  t  o  f  e  t  c  h  a  p  a  a  i  l  o  f
x  w  a  t  e  b  o  x  e  s  r  j  x  a  c  k  o
e  f  t  a  x  e  s  e  l  l  d  o  e  w  n  a  x
s  n  d  b  r  o  k  e  h  i  s  c  s  r  o  w  e
n  a  n  d  j  f  i  x  e  s  i  l  l  c  a  m  s
e  t  u  m  b  l  i  n  g  a  x  e  s  a  f  t  e
r  t  h  e  n  j  s  t  r  i  p  e  a  c  k  g  o
s  i  x  e  s  t  u  p  a  n  d  h  o  v  i  n  e
```

B. Match each spelling word with the right clue.

_____ 1. sixes   a. repairs or makes something right

_____ 2. mixes   b. tools for chopping wood

_____ 3. axes   c. polishes for cars and furniture

_____ 4. taxes   d. cardboard containers

_____ 5. waxes   e. numbers

_____ 6. fixes   f. furry-tailed animals

_____ 7. foxes   g. blends

_____ 8. boxes   h. money we pay the government

Name _____

Words with *-xes*

boxes	fixes	taxes	mixes
foxes	waxes	axes	sixes

A. Put an *X* on the word that is <u>not</u> the same.

1. boxes	doxes	boxes	boxes	boxes
2. foxes	foxes	foxes	toxes	foxes
3. fixes	fixes	fizes	fixes	fixes
4. waxes	maxes	waxes	waxes	waxes
5. taxes	taxes	taxes	faxes	taxes
6. axes	axes	axes	axes	oxes
7. mixes	mixes	mixes	wixes	mixes

B. Write the words that can be either nouns or verbs.

1. _____   2. _____   3. _____

4. _____   5. _____

C. Use spelling words to complete the puzzle.

Across

1. He ___ the floor each week.

4. containers

5. the numbers after the fives

Down

2. chopping tools

3. animals

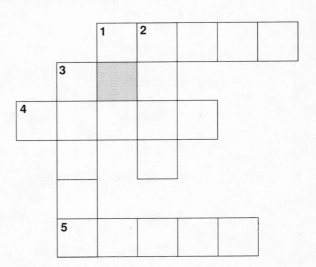

LESSON 22 Words with *-ches*

branches	stitches	churches	crutches
speeches	scratches	catches	matches

A. Fill in each blank with a spelling word.

1. The dog _____ at its fleas.

2. The outfielder _____ the ball.

3. We will need some _____ to light the fire.

4. The president makes many _____ each year.

5. The cut on my hand needed _____.

6. The strong winds broke the tree's _____.

7. He had to use _____ until his leg mended.

8. I like to visit old _____.

B. Circle the letters that are the same in all the words.

branches	speeches	stitches	scratches
churches	catches	crutches	matches

C. Write a spelling word under each picture.

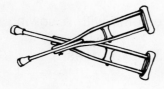  

1. _____ 2. _____ 3. _____

D. Find the missing letters. Then write the word.

1. c ___ u t ___ ___ e s _____

2. s t ___ ___ ___ e s _____

Name _____

Words with *-ches*

branches	stitches	churches	crutches
speeches	scratches	catches	matches

A. Find the hidden words on the list.

branches	scratches	crutches	bite
speeches	churches	matches	drive
stitches	catches	wise	why

```
c  a  t  c  h  e  s  o  s  l  d  k  i  n  g  c  o  s
l  e  w  a  s  a  m  e  c  r  u  t  c  h  e  s  r  p
r  y  o  l  e  s  o  u  r  l  a  n  d  a  m  e  r  e
m  a  t  c  h  e  s  r  a  y  d  r  i  v  e  w  o  e
l  e  s  o  u  l  w  a  t  s  h  e  h  e  c  i  a  c
l  l  e  d  f  o  r  h  c  h  u  r  c  h  e  s  i  h
s  t  i  t  c  h  e  s  h  s  p  i  b  i  t  e  p  e
h  e  c  a  l  l  e  d  e  f  o  r  h  i  s  b  o  s
w  l  a  n  d  h  e  c  s  a  l  w  h  y  l  e  d  f
o  r  b  r  a  n  c  h  e  s  h  i  s  f  i  d  d  l
```

B. Match each spelling word with the right clue.

_____ 1. stitches   **a.** the parts of a tree that have leaves

_____ 2. scratches   **b.** in-and-out movements with a sewing needle

_____ 3. churches   **c.** what a baseball player does

_____ 4. catches   **d.** houses of worship

_____ 5. crutches   **e.** marks made by a cat's claws

_____ 6. matches   **f.** talks given to an audience

_____ 7. branches   **g.** used for support if a leg is broken

_____ 8. speeches   **h.** used for starting fires

Words with *-ches*

branches	stitches	churches	crutches
speeches	scratches	catches	matches

A. Put an *X* on the word that is <u>not</u> the same.

1. branches	branches	brenches	branches	branches
2. speeches	speeches	speeches	squeeches	speeches
3. stitches	stitshes	stitches	stitches	stitches
4. scratches	scratches	scretches	scratches	scratches
5. churches	churches	churches	churches	charches
6. catches	catches	catches	cotches	catches
7. crutches	cnutches	crutches	crutches	crutches
8. matches	matches	watches	matches	matches

B. Write the spelling words in alphabetical order.

1. _____ 2. _____ 3. _____ 4. _____

5. _____ 6. _____ 7. _____ 8. _____

C. Use spelling words to complete the story.

My sisters and friends and I were at a Fourth of July picnic. We listened

to _____. Then we ate lunch with our families. We had fried chicken

and chocolate cake. It was great!

Then we climbed the trees. We were playing on the _____ when

the limbs broke and we all fell. Most of us got only _____. But one

girl had to get _____. Another friend had to use _____ to

walk for the next month.

Name _____

Words with -ches

branches	stitches	churches	crutches
speeches	scratches	catches	matches

A. Write the simplest form of each spelling word.

1. _____ 2. _____ 3. _____ 4. _____

5. _____ 6. _____ 7. _____ 8. _____

B. Match each spelling word with a related word.

_____ **1.** branches   **a.** doctor

_____ **2.** speeches   **b.** ball

_____ **3.** stitches   **c.** tree

_____ **4.** scratches   **d.** president

_____ **5.** churches   **e.** broken leg

_____ **6.** catches   **f.** weddings

_____ **7.** crutches   **g.** cat

C. Use each spelling word in a sentence.

branches _____

speeches _____

stitches _____

scratches _____

churches _____

catches   _____

crutches _____

matches   _____

Words with -ies

pennies	cherries	ponies	cities
babies	berries	puppies	guppies

A. Fill in each blank with a spelling word.

1. New York, Chicago, and Dallas are very large _____.

2. Currants are small, sour _____.

3. The _____ on the tree look ripe to me.

4. Small horses are called _____.

5. _____ make good fish for your aquarium.

6. The dog had five _____.

7. A nursery is where you'll find _____.

8. I'll trade you a dime for ten _____.

B. Circle the letters that are the same in all the words.

pennies   babies   cherries   berries   ponies   puppies   cities   guppies

C. Change the plural *ies* in the spelling words to the singular ending *y*. Write the singular words in the blanks.

Plural	Singular
1. pennies	_____
2. babies	_____
3. cherries	_____
4. berries	_____
5. ponies	_____
6. puppies	_____
7. cities	_____

© 1991 Steck-Vaughn Company. Target 780

Name _____

LESSON 23

Words with *-ies*

pennies	cherries	ponies	cities
babies	berries	puppies	guppies

A. Use spelling words to complete the story.

One spring I went to Mexico. Most of the towns and _____ have street markets. Anything you might want to buy can be found there. There are long rows of stalls. Some stalls sell food. For just _____ you can buy _____, grapes, or other fruit.

Some rows sell animals that you can buy for pets. I saw some of the cutest _____ I've ever seen. One man even had _____ for little kids to ride.

B. Write the words that name things you can touch.

1. _____ 2. _____ 3. _____ 4. _____

5. _____ 6. _____ 7. _____ 8. _____

C. Match each spelling word with a related word.

_____ 1. pennies   **a.** horses

_____ 2. babies   **b.** money

_____ 3. cherries   **c.** traffic

_____ 4. berries   **d.** crib

_____ 5. ponies   **e.** water

_____ 6. puppies   **f.** seeds

_____ 7. cities   **g.** pits

_____ 8. guppies   **h.** dogs

90

Words with *-ies*

| pennies | cherries | ponies | cities |
| babies | berries | puppies | guppies |

A. Use spelling words to complete the puzzle.

Across

3. small fish

6. big towns

7. very young children

Down

1. baby dogs

2. red fruits with pits

4. cents

5. small horses

B. Write a spelling word under each picture.

1. _____   2. _____   3. _____

Name _____

LESSON 23   Words with -ies

| pennies | cherries | ponies | cities |
| babies | berries | puppies | guppies |

A. Fill in the boxes with the right words.

1.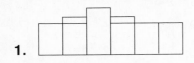

2.

3.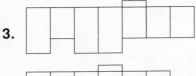

4.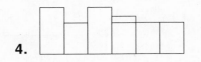

5.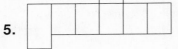

6.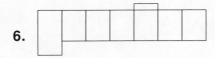

B. Complete these exercises with spelling words.

1. Write three words that can be pets.

_____ _____ _____

2. Write two words that are fruits.

_____ _____

3. Write the only word that contains the letter *a*. _____

4. Write the word that describes a place where people live. _____

5. Write the word for a type of money. _____

6. Write the word that begins with two consonants. _____

7. Write the only word that contains the letter *o*. _____

8. Write the words that have three different vowels.

_____ _____

_____ _____

LESSON 24

Homonyms

hare	tail	sew	heal
hair	tale	sow	heel

A. Fill in each blank with a spelling word.

1. I had to get a new _____ put on my shoe.

2. A _____ is a larger kind of rabbit.

3. Do you ever play "Pin the _____ on the donkey"?

4. My uncle told me a _____ about his younger days.

5. We will _____ the corn seed in the field today.

6. Can you _____ a button on your shirt?

7. The cut will take a while to _____.

8. I love to feel the wind through my _____.

B. Circle the right answers.

1. "Sew" and "sow" are not spelled the same, but they

     sound alike.   mean the same.   smell the same.

2. The words in your lesson are

     homonyms.   antonyms.   synonyms.

3. To "heal" is to

     cure.   fight.   follow.

C. Find the missing letters. Then write the word.

1. t ___ i ___   _____

2. ___ o ___   _____

Name _____

Homonyms

hare	tail	sew	heal
hair	tale	sow	heel

A. Write the spelling words that rhyme with the words below.

1. jail   rail   _____

2. know   so   _____

3. feel   meal   _____

4. care   dare   _____

5. crow   low   _____

B. Put an X on the word that is not the same.

1. hare	hane	hare	hare	hare
2. hair	hair	hair	hair	hain
3. tail	tail	fail	tail	tail
4. tale	tale	tele	tale	tale
5. sew	sew	sew	sow	sew
6. sow	sow	sow	osw	sow
7. heal	heal	heal	heal	hael
8. heel	heel	heel	beel	heel

C. Write a spelling word under each picture.

1. _____   **2.** _____   **3.** _____

LESSON 24   Homonyms

hare	tail	sew	heal
hair	tale	sow	heel

A. Match each spelling word with the right clue.

_____ **1.** heel   **a.** to plant seeds

_____ **2.** sow   **b.** an animal with long ears, a divided upper lip, and long hind legs for leaping

_____ **3.** tale   **c.** to make healthy again

_____ **4.** hair   **d.** the back part of the foot

_____ **5.** hare   **e.** to join by stitches

_____ **6.** tail   **f.** a story

_____ **7.** sew   **g.** the bottom or end part of something

_____ **8.** heal   **h.** fiber or fur

B. Write the words that name things you can touch.

1. _____   **2.** _____   **3.** _____   **4.** _____

C. Write the spelling words in alphabetical order.

1. _____   **2.** _____   **3.** _____   **4.** _____

5. _____   **6.** _____   **7.** _____   **8.** _____

D. Fill in the boxes with the right words.

1.    **2.**   **3.**

4. 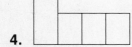   **5.**   **6.**

Name _____

Homonyms

hare	tail	sew	heal
hair	tale	sow	heel

A. **Use spelling words to complete the story.**

Once upon a time there was a sly _____. This hare lived on a farm and loved it. He had a nice and cozy hole for a home. He had plenty of vegetables from the fields to eat. His favorite hobby was to play games and make the farmer mad.

One day the farmer spied the hare in the carrot patch. He crept toward the hare and reached out to grab the hare's _____. But the hare hopped away. This made the farmer so mad, he chased the hare across the field. The farmer tripped and fell, tearing his shirt. "You pesky hare!" cried the farmer. "Now I'll have to _____ my shirt back together." But the hare didn't hear the farmer. He was safely back in his hole.

B. **Use each spelling word in a sentence.**

hare _____

hair _____

tail _____

tale _____

sew _____

sow _____

heal _____

heel _____

Words with *-ves*

leaves	knives	shelves	loaves
wolves	calves	thieves	lives

A. Fill in each blank with a spelling word.

1. The cowboys caught the horse _____.

2. Can you help me put the books on the _____?

3. All the _____ in our kitchen are very sharp.

4. Three of our cows had _____.

5. How many _____ of bread did you buy at the store?

6. When fall comes, the _____ always pile up in the yard.

7. Many _____ were saved by the firefighters.

8. _____ are not mean animals as some people think.

B. Circle the letters that are the same in all the words.

leaves   wolves   knives   calves   shelves   thieves   loaves   lives

C. Write the singular form of the spelling words.

1. _____   2. _____   3. _____   4. _____

5. _____   6. _____   7. _____   8. _____

D. Find the missing letters. Then write the word.

1. ___ o l ___ ___ ___   _____

2. ___ e ___ ___ e s   _____

3. ___ ___ i e ___ ___ ___   _____

4. l ___ ___ ___ ___   _____

Name _____

97

Words with *-ves*

leaves	knives	shelves	loaves
wolves	calves	thieves	lives

A. **Use spelling words to complete the story.**

Someone who _____ his or her home to find a new home is

called a settler. Many years ago, the _____ of most settlers were

hard. They had to build their own houses. They grew all their own food.

They also had to protect themselves from _____ and bandits.

Sometimes they even had to fight off bears and _____.

B. **Write a spelling word under each picture.**

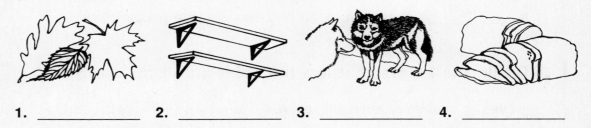

1. _____ 2. _____ 3. _____ 4. _____

C. **One word is wrong in each sentence. Circle the wrong word. Then fill in the blank with a spelling word that makes sense.**

1. We have to rake snow in the fall.   _____

2. Please put the books on the top lamps.   _____

3. We set the table with forks and hammers.   _____

4. We bought ten quarts of bread for the picnic.   _____

5. The scouts robbed the bank of all its money.   _____

6. The firefighters saved many flowers in the rescue. _____

Words with *-ves*

leaves	knives	shelves	loaves
wolves	calves	thieves	lives

A. Find the hidden words on the list.

leaves	calves	loaves	know
wolves	shelves	lives	pole
knives	thieves	home	stone

```
h e y d i d l d l e c d i d l d l
e t h s e c e a t a a n d p o l e
t w h h e f a i d d l e t h a e c
h o m e o w v j u m v p e d v o v
e l r l t h e m k o e k o n e t h
e v l v i t s t n l s n e d s o g
l e a e u g h e o d l i v e s t o
s s e s e s u c w h s v p o r t a
n d t h i e v e s t h e d i s h r
a n a w a y w i t h t s t o n e h
```

B. Match each spelling word with a related word.

_____ **1.** leaves   **a.** barn

_____ **2.** wolves   **b.** rake

_____ **3.** knives   **c.** steal

_____ **4.** calves   **d.** bread

_____ **5.** shelves   **e.** pack

_____ **6.** thieves   **f.** cut

_____ **7.** loaves   **g.** books

_____ **8.** lives   **h.** births

Name _____

LESSON 25   Words with *-ves*

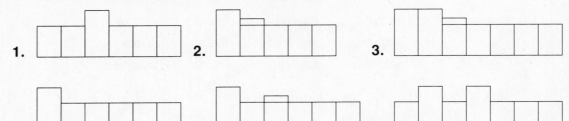

leaves   knives   shelves   loaves

wolves   calves   thieves   lives

A. Fill in the boxes with the right words.

1.
2.
3.

4.
5.
6.

B. Complete these exercises with spelling words.

1. Which words have the long *e* sound?

   _____   _____

2. Which word has five consonants? _____

3. Which words have the letter *o* in them?

   _____   _____

C. Use spelling words to complete the puzzle.

Across

2. They hold books.

4. wild animals

Down

1. robbers

3. Bread comes in ___.

LESSON 26

Words with *-sses*

dresses	illnesses	glasses	kisses
bosses	classes	guesses	losses

A. Fill in each blank with a spelling word.

1. Doctors learn how to treat many _____.

2. At school I go to art and reading _____.

3. I broke my _____ and can't see very well.

4. He works for two _____ at his job.

5. Her closet is full of new _____.

6. Some people greet each other with _____ on the cheek.

7. The man at the carnival _____ your weight.

8. The team had many wins and few _____.

B. Circle the letters that are the same in all the words.

dresses bosses illnesses classes glasses guesses kisses losses

C. Write the singular form of the spelling words.

1. _____   2. _____   3. _____   4. _____

5. _____   6. _____   7. _____   8. _____

D. Fill in the boxes with the right words.

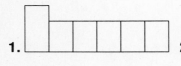

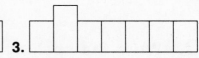
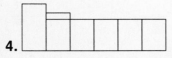
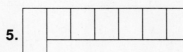
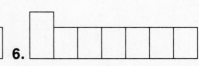

Name _____

LESSON 26

Words with -sses

dresses	illnesses	glasses	kisses
bosses	classes	guesses	losses

A. Use spelling words to complete the story.

When I was fifteen, we moved from Texas to New York. I was scared my
first day of school there. It felt funny not knowing anyone. But the kids in all
my _____ were nice. They asked me where I was from. I said
slowly, "I'll give y'all three _____."

Everyone _____ the same in New York as in Texas. They
like the same music and play the same sports. I played on a great baseball
team. We had almost no _____.

When we moved back to Texas, I left behind many good friends in New
York. I hope to go back there again one day.

B. Write a spelling word under each picture.

1. _____ 2. _____ 3. _____ 4. _____

C. Write the spelling words in alphabetical order.

1. _____ 2. _____ 3. _____ 4. _____

5. _____ 6. _____ 7. _____ 8. _____

102

Words with -sses

dresses	illnesses	glasses	kisses
bosses	classes	guesses	losses

A. Put an X on the word that is not the same.

1. dresses	dresses	dresses	dresses	tresses
2. bosses	bosses	bosses	dosses	bosses
3. illnesses	illmesses	illnesses	illnesses	illnesses
4. classes	classes	classes	closses	classes
5. glasses	glasses	glasses	glasses	glases
6. guesses	guesses	geusses	guesses	guesses

B. Match each spelling word with the right clue.

_____ 1. losses   **a.** puts on clothes

_____ 2. kisses   **b.** leaders or chiefs

_____ 3. guesses   **c.** containers for drinks

_____ 4. glasses   **d.** sicknesses

_____ 5. classes   **e.** things that are lost

_____ 6. illnesses   **f.** partners of hugs

_____ 7. bosses   **g.** what someone who doesn't know the answer does

_____ 8. dresses   **h.** learning places

C. Find the missing letters. Then write the word.

1. g l ____ ____ ____ e s   _____

2. l ____ s s ____ ____   _____

Name _____

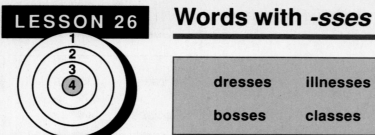

Words with *-sses*

dresses	illnesses	glasses	kisses
bosses	classes	guesses	losses

A. Use spelling words to complete the puzzle.

Across

4. sicknesses

5. gets dressed

6. chiefs

Down

1. You get three ___.

2. hugs and ___

3. They help you see better.

B. Use each spelling word in a sentence.

dresses _____

bosses _____

illnesses _____

classes _____

glasses _____

guesses _____

kisses _____

losses _____

Irregular plural words

men	children	mice	sheep
women	teeth	oxen	geese

A. Fill in each blank with a spelling word.

1. Cats love to chase _____.

2. Some farmers use _____ to pull their plows.

3. My dentist says my _____ are healthy and clean.

4. _____ fly in flocks and make honking sounds.

5. The wool for my sweater comes from _____.

6. Some games and toys aren't just for _____.

7. Boys grow up to become _____.

8. Girls grow up to become _____.

B. Write the singular form of the spelling words. Use a dictionary for help.

Plural	Singular		Plural	Singular
1. men	_____		5. mice	_____
2. women	_____		6. oxen	_____
3. children	_____		7. sheep	_____
4. teeth	_____		8. geese	_____

C. Write the spelling words in alphabetical order.

1. _____ 2. _____ 3. _____ 4. _____

5. _____ 6. _____ 7. _____ 8. _____

Name _____

Irregular plural words

men	children	mice	sheep
women	teeth	oxen	geese

A. Write the spelling words that rhyme with the words below.

1. hen   ten   _____

2. deep   keep   _____

3. dice   rice   _____

4. piece   lease   _____

B. Write a spelling word under each picture.

1. _____   2. _____   3. _____   4. _____

C. Use spelling words to complete the story.

My friend is a special kind of doctor. She doesn't take care of grown-ups

and _____. She treats their pets.

Most of the time she cares for dogs, cats, birds, hamsters, and

_____. She gives them their shots, makes them well when they're

sick, and cleans their _____.

Her partner works with large animals that live on farms. He sees horses,

cattle, and even ducks and _____.

I like to visit their office. One time a man came in with a pet raccoon.

Another time someone brought in a pet snake.

Irregular plural words

men	children	mice	sheep
women	teeth	oxen	geese

A. Find the hidden words on the list.

men	teeth	sheep	rose
women	mice	geese	note
children	oxen	slope	drove

```
l  s  h  e  e  p  o  n  d  o  n  b  w  r  i  d  g
e  i  s  f  a  l  l  i  n  g  d  o  o  x  e  n  w
n  g  f  r  o  s  e  a  l  l  i  n  m  e  n  g  d
o  e  w  n  l  o  n  d  s  o  n  t  e  b  r  i  d
g  e  i  s  f  c  h  i  l  d  r  e  n  a  l  l  i
n  s  g  d  o  w  n  m  o  y  f  e  a  i  r  l  a
d  e  y  n  b  u  i  l  p  d  i  t  u  p  w  i  t
h  d  r  o  v  e  w  o  e  o  d  h  a  n  d  c  l
a  y  w  t  o  o  d  a  n  d  c  l  a  y  b  u  i
l  d  i  e  t  u  p  m  i  c  e  w  i  t  h  w  e
```

B. Match each spelling word with a related word.

_____	1. men	**a.**	cats
_____	2. women	**b.**	shepherd
_____	3. children	**c.**	kindergarten
_____	4. teeth	**d.**	plows
_____	5. mice	**e.**	boys
_____	6. oxen	**f.**	"honk"
_____	7. sheep	**g.**	girls
_____	8. geese	**h.**	mouth

Name_____

Irregular plural words

men	children	mice	sheep
women	teeth	oxen	geese

A. Fill in the boxes with the right words.

1.

2.

3.

4.

5.

6.

B. Complete these exercises with spelling words.

1. Which word has the most letters? _____

2. Which word has three *e*'s? _____

3. Which is the shortest word? _____

C. Use spelling words to complete the puzzle.

Across

4. more than one goose

5. more than one sheep

6. more than one woman

Down

1. more than one tooth

2. more than one man

3. more than one child

108

Homonyms

know	write	hour	son
no	right	our	sun

A. Fill in each blank with a spelling word.

1. Will you _____ to me while you're at camp?

2. We're proud of _____ new car.

3. My sister's _____ is my nephew.

4. Do you _____ how to count change?

5. It takes an _____ to ride the bus home.

6. The teacher said, "Your answer is _____."

7. I have _____ idea how my pet snake escaped.

8. The _____ is our brightest star.

B. Circle the right answers.

1. "Write" and "right" sound alike, but they

   mean the same.   are not spelled the same.   look the same.

2. The words in this lesson are

   antonyms.   homonyms.   synonyms.

C. Find the missing letters. Then write the word.

1. ___ o u ___   _____

2. ___ ___ o w   _____

D. Write the spelling words in alphabetical order.

1. _____ 2. _____ 3. _____ 4. _____

5. _____ 6. _____ 7. _____ 8. _____

© 1991 Steck-Vaughn Company. Target 780

Name _____

Homonyms

know	write	hour	son
no	right	our	sun

A. Write the spelling words that rhyme with the words below.

1. ton   fun   _____

2. light   fight   _____

3. flour   tower   _____

B. Put an *X* on the word that is <u>not</u> the same.

1. know	know	know	krow	know
2. no	on	no	no	no
3. write	write	wrife	write	write
4. right	right	righf	right	right
5. hour	hour	hour	hour	houn
6. our	our	our	oun	our

C. Match each spelling word with a related word.

_____ **1.** son   **a.** moon

_____ **2.** sun   **b.** your

_____ **3.** hour   **c.** yes

_____ **4.** our   **d.** pencil

_____ **5.** right   **e.** daughter

_____ **6.** write   **f.** minute

_____ **7.** know   **g.** left

_____ **8.** no   **h.** understand

Homonyms

know	write	hour	son
no	right	our	sun

A. Use spelling words to complete the story.

Long ago, a man and his _____ were held in a prison tower.

They wanted to escape. The father observed the flight of birds and would

_____ down what he saw.

He made wax and took feathers from the birds to make huge wings.

At just the right _____, they put on the wings. Then they flew

from the tower over the sea. They wanted to fly to a nearby island.

The father flew a straight course. But the boy got excited and flew too

high. The _____ melted the wax on his wings. He fell into the

ocean. The father reached the island but he cried for the loss of his son.

B. Write a spelling word under each picture.

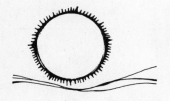   

1. _____ 2. _____ 3. _____ 4. _____

C. Write the words that name things you cannot touch.

1. _____ 2. _____ 3. _____ 4. _____

5. _____ 6. _____ 7. _____

Name _____

Homonyms

know	write	hour	son
no	right	our	sun

A. Fill in the boxes with the right words.

1.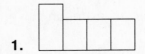

2.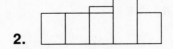

3.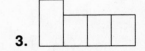

4.

5.

6.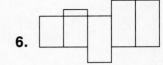

B. Complete these exercises with spelling words.

1. Which words begin with a silent letter?

   _____   _____   _____

2. Which words contain the letter *u*?

   _____   _____   _____

3. Which word contains a silent *gh*? _____

4. Which word is the shortest? _____

5. Which words contain the letter *i*? _____   _____

C. Use each spelling word in a sentence.

know _____

no _____

write _____

right _____

hour _____

our _____

Compound words with *any-*

anyone	anybody	anyhow	anyway
anything	anyplace	anywhere	anytime

A. Fill in each blank with a spelling word.

1. There are _____ from three to five possums living under our house.

2. _____ you can do, I can do better!

3. I don't know _____ by that name.

4. He can come to my house _____ he wants.

5. What do you want to do that for, _____?

6. You can put the box _____ you like.

7. Is there _____ here who speaks Spanish?

8. I'm going _____, even if she's not.

B. Circle the letters that are the same in all the words.

anyone   anything   anybody   anyplace   anytime

C. Circle the right answers.

1. All of the spelling words are called

   contractions.   compacts.   compounds.

2. All of the spelling words have

   one syllable.   more than one syllable.

D. Find the missing letters. Then write the word.

1. a n y t ___ ___ ___   _____

2. a n y w ___ ___   _____

Name _____

Compound words with *any-*

anyone	anybody	anyhow	anyway
anything	anyplace	anywhere	anytime

A. Put an *X* on the word that is <u>not</u> the same.

1. anyone	anyone	anynoe	anyone	anyone
2. anything	anything	anything	anything	anythiny
3. anybody	anybody	anyboby	anybody	anybody
4. anyplace	anyglace	anyplace	anyplace	anyplace
5. anyhow	anyhow	anyhow	anyhow	anybow
6. anywhere	anywhere	anywheer	anywhere	anywhere
7. anyway	anymay	anyway	anyway	anyway
8. anytime	anytime	anyfime	anytime	anytime

B. Write the spelling words in alphabetical order.

1. _____   2. _____   3. _____   4. _____

5. _____   6. _____   7. _____   8. _____

C. Use spelling words to complete the story.

There are times when I can't make up my mind. My friend called and

asked what I wanted to do. "Oh, _____ is fine with me," I told

him. He asked where I wanted to meet him. "_____ you choose

is all right," I said.

"What time shall we meet?" my friend asked.

"_____ that suits you," I answered.

Compound words with *any-*

anyone	anybody	anyhow	anyway
anything	anyplace	anywhere	anytime

A. Find the hidden words on the list.

anyone	anyplace	anyway	don't
anything	anyhow	anytime	fair
anybody	anywhere	own	chair

```
a  n  y  t  i  m  e  t  h  e  r  e  w  a  s  a  a
n  l  i  t  t  l  e  g  a  n  y  b  o  d  y  i  n
y  r  i  w  h  o  h  a  d  a  l  i  t  t  f  l  y
w  e  a  n  y  o  n  e  c  u  o  w  n  r  a  l  t
a  r  i  g  h  t  i  n  c  h  a  i  r  t  i  h  h
y  e  m  d  i  d  d  l  e  o  f  h  e  r  r  f  i
o  r  e  o  h  e  a  n  y  p  l  a  c  e  a  n  n
w  h  e  n  s  h  e  w  a  s  g  o  o  d  s  h  g
e  w  a  t  s  v  e  r  y  v  e  r  y  g  o  o  d
a  n  y  h  o  w  a  n  d  a  n  y  w  h  e  r  e
```

B. Complete these exercises with spelling words.

1. Write two words about people. _____ _____

2. Write two words about places. _____ _____

3. Write one word about time. _____

C. Match the spelling word with the word that is nearly the same.

_____ 1. anybody   **a.** whenever

_____ 2. anytime   **b.** whatever

_____ 3. anything   **c.** whoever

Name _____

Compound words with *any-*

anyone	anybody	anyhow	anyway
anything	anyplace	anywhere	anytime

A. Make as many new words from each spelling word as you can.

1. anyone = *any*   *one*   *none*   *an*

2. anything = _____ _____ _____ _____

3. anybody = _____ _____ _____ _____

4. anyplace = _____ _____ _____ _____

5. anyhow = _____ _____ _____ _____

6. anywhere = _____ _____ _____ _____

7. anyway = _____ _____ _____ _____

8. anytime = _____ _____ _____ _____

B. Use spelling words to complete the puzzle.

Across

2. Can ___ hear me?

3. Is there ___ I can do?

4. anyway

Down

1. anyhow

2. ___ can come to the party.

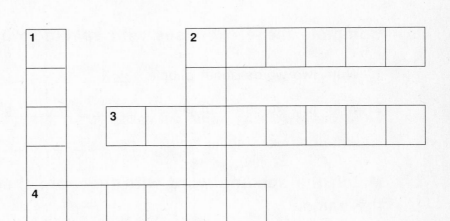

Compound words with *some-*

someone	somebody	somehow	sometime
something	someplace	somewhere	someday

A. Fill in each blank with a spelling word.

1. _____ he was able to lift the car.

2. I would like to go to town _____ today.

3. This sunset is _____ to see!

4. I hope to visit Rome _____.

5. Let's go _____ and talk.

6. Can _____ help us?

7. _____ is looking for you over there.

8. In *The Wizard of Oz*, there is a song called "_____ Over the Rainbow."

B. Circle the letters that are the same in all the words.

someone   something   somebody   someplace

somehow   somewhere   sometime   someday

C. Circle the right answers.

1. All of the spelling words are called

    contractions.   compounds.   compacts.

2. All of the spelling words have

    one syllable.   more than one syllable.

D. Find the missing letters. Then write the word.

s o m e h ___ ___   _____

Name _____

Compound words with *some-*

someone	somebody	somehow	sometime
something	someplace	somewhere	someday

A. Put an *X* on the word that is <u>not</u> the same.

1. someone	someone	someoue	someone	someone
2. something	something	something	sowething	something
3. somebody	somedoby	somebody	somebody	somebody
4. someplace	someplace	someplace	someplace	someqlace
5. somehow	somebow	somehow	somehow	somehow
6. somewhere	somewhere	somewhere	somemhere	somewhere
7. sometime	sometime	sowetime	sometime	sometime
8. someday	someday	someday	someday	somebay

B. Write the spelling words in alphabetical order.

1. _____   2. _____   3. _____

4. _____   5. _____   6. _____

7. _____   8. _____

C. Use spelling words to complete the story.

There are those in the world who are _____ able to write

great songs. One such song is "_____ Over the Rainbow."

Writing the words to a song is a lot like writing a poem. But then you

have to add music. It must be a hard thing to do. I think there's

_____ magic about how a song comes about. Maybe I'll write a

great song _____.

Compound words with *some-*

someone	somebody	somehow	sometime
something	someplace	somewhere	someday

A. Find the hidden words on the list.

someone	someplace	sometime	spare
something	somehow	someday	tear
somebody	somewhere	care	right

```
s  i  s  o  m  e  h  o  w  m  c  s  p  s  l  e  s  s
i  m  o  n  m  e  t  a  p  i  a  o  e  o  m  a  n  o
s  o  m  e  w  h  e  r  e  g  r  m  o  m  i  n  g  m
t  o  t  h  s  o  m  e  o  n  e  e  e  e  f  a  i  e
r  s  a  i  d  s  i  m  p  l  e  t  s  t  e  a  r  b
i  m  o  n  t  o  t  h  e  p  i  i  e  h  m  a  i  o
s  o  m  e  p  l  a  c  e  n  l  m  e  i  t  m  g  d
e  t  a  k  e  y  o  u  t  h  e  e  r  n  e  s  h  y
i  n  g  s  o  m  e  d  a  y  a  s  o  g  n  g  t  o
f  s  i  x  p  e  n  c  e  a  p  s  p  a  r  e  o  c
```

B. Complete these exercises with spelling words.

1. Write two words about people: _____ _____

2. Write two words about places: _____ _____

3. Write two words about time: _____ _____

C. Match each spelling word with its opposite word.

_____ 1. someday   **a.** nobody

_____ 2. someplace   **b.** never

_____ 3. somebody   **c.** nowhere

Name _____

Compound words with *some-*

someone	somebody	somehow	sometime
something	someplace	somewhere	someday

A. Make as many new words from each spelling word as you can.

1. someone = *some*   *one*   *me*   *so*

2. something = _____ _____ _____ _____

3. somebody = _____ _____ _____ _____

4. someplace = _____ _____ _____ _____

5. somehow = _____ _____ _____ _____

6. somewhere = _____ _____ _____ _____

7. sometime = _____ _____ _____ _____

8. someday = _____ _____ _____ _____

B. Use spelling words to complete the puzzle.

Across

1. on a later day

2. someplace

3. Is ___ wrong?

4. somewhere

Down

1. Come see me ___.

2. I'll find a way ___.

My Word List

Words I Can Spell

Put a ✓ in the box beside each word you spell correctly on your weekly test.

1

- [ ] her
- [ ] fern
- [ ] jerk
- [ ] nerve
- [ ] perch
- [ ] verb
- [ ] herd
- [ ] perk

2

- [ ] burst
- [ ] turn
- [ ] burn
- [ ] nurse
- [ ] church
- [ ] curve
- [ ] purse
- [ ] curb

3

- [ ] launch
- [ ] gauze
- [ ] vault
- [ ] haul
- [ ] fault
- [ ] cause
- [ ] haunt
- [ ] August

4

- [ ] red
- [ ] read
- [ ] not
- [ ] knot
- [ ] maid
- [ ] made
- [ ] be
- [ ] bee

5

- [ ] crawl
- [ ] lawn
- [ ] dawn
- [ ] yawn
- [ ] brawl
- [ ] claw
- [ ] flaw
- [ ] straw

Words To Review

If you miss a word on your test, write it here. Practice it until you can spell it correctly. Then check the box beside the word.

_____

_____

_____

_____

_____

_____

_____

_____

_____

_____

_____

_____

_____

_____

_____

_____

Name _____

My Word List

Words I Can Spell

Put a ✓ in the box beside each word you spell correctly on your weekly test.

6

- ☐ foot
- ☐ hook
- ☐ wood
- ☐ brook
- ☐ stood
- ☐ hood
- ☐ crook
- ☐ cook

7

- ☐ food
- ☐ noon
- ☐ bloom
- ☐ loose
- ☐ booth
- ☐ tooth
- ☐ goose
- ☐ proof

8

- ☐ thief
- ☐ chief
- ☐ niece
- ☐ piece
- ☐ field
- ☐ shield
- ☐ brief
- ☐ yield

9

- ☐ road
- ☐ rode
- ☐ pail
- ☐ pale
- ☐ ate
- ☐ eight
- ☐ see
- ☐ sea

10

- ☐ breath
- ☐ spread
- ☐ thread
- ☐ ready
- ☐ feather
- ☐ heavy
- ☐ weather
- ☐ leather

Words To Review

If you miss a word on your test, write it here. Practice it until you can spell it correctly. Then check the box beside the word.

My Word List

Words I Can Spell

Put a ✓ in the box beside each word you spell correctly on your weekly test.

11

☐ heard   ☐ earth
☐ learn   ☐ search
☐ earn   ☐ hearse
☐ pearl   ☐ early

12

☐ cry   ☐ fly
☐ fry   ☐ sky
☐ dry   ☐ spy
☐ shy   ☐ pry

13

☐ to   ☐ bear
☐ two   ☐ bare
☐ for   ☐ flour
☐ four   ☐ flower

14

☐ sleigh   ☐ neighbor
☐ freight   ☐ neigh
☐ weigh   ☐ eighty
☐ weight   ☐ freighter

15

☐ kneel   ☐ knot
☐ knock   ☐ knob
☐ knife   ☐ knight
☐ knit   ☐ knack

Words To Review

If you miss a word on your test, write it here. Practice it until you can spell it correctly. Then check the box beside the word.

_____
_____
_____
_____
_____
_____
_____
_____
_____
_____
_____
_____
_____
_____
_____
_____
_____

Name _____

My Word List

Words I Can Spell

Put a ✓ in the box beside each word you spell correctly on your weekly test.

16

☐ wrench   ☐ wreck
☐ wring   ☐ wrestle
☐ wrist   ☐ wren
☐ wrong   ☐ wreath

17

☐ won't   ☐ didn't
☐ aren't   ☐ wasn't
☐ isn't   ☐ hasn't
☐ doesn't   ☐ weren't

18

☐ blew   ☐ sale
☐ blue   ☐ sail
☐ hear   ☐ knew
☐ here   ☐ new

19

☐ I'll   ☐ I've
☐ you'll   ☐ you've
☐ she'll   ☐ we've
☐ he'll   ☐ they've

20

☐ bushes   ☐ brushes
☐ wishes   ☐ dishes
☐ crushes   ☐ washes
☐ flashes   ☐ fishes

Words To Review

If you miss a word on your test, write it here. Practice it until you can spell it correctly. Then check the box beside the word.

My Word List

Words I Can Spell

Put a ✓ in the box beside each word you spell correctly on your weekly test.

21

- ☐ boxes
- ☐ foxes
- ☐ fixes
- ☐ waxes
- ☐ taxes
- ☐ axes
- ☐ mixes
- ☐ sixes

22

- ☐ branches
- ☐ speeches
- ☐ stitches
- ☐ scratches
- ☐ churches
- ☐ catches
- ☐ crutches
- ☐ matches

23

- ☐ pennies
- ☐ babies
- ☐ cherries
- ☐ berries
- ☐ ponies
- ☐ puppies
- ☐ cities
- ☐ guppies

24

- ☐ hare
- ☐ hair
- ☐ tail
- ☐ tale
- ☐ sew
- ☐ sow
- ☐ heal
- ☐ heel

25

- ☐ leaves
- ☐ wolves
- ☐ knives
- ☐ calves
- ☐ shelves
- ☐ thieves
- ☐ loaves
- ☐ lives

Words To Review

If you miss a word on your test, write it here. Practice it until you can spell it correctly. Then check the box beside the word.

_____

_____

_____

_____

_____

_____

_____

_____

_____

_____

_____

_____

_____

_____

_____

_____

Name _____

My Word List

Words I Can Spell

Put a ✓ in the box beside each word you spell correctly on your weekly test.

26

☐	dresses	☐	glasses
☐	bosses	☐	guesses
☐	illnesses	☐	kisses
☐	classes	☐	losses

27

☐	men	☐	mice
☐	women	☐	oxen
☐	children	☐	sheep
☐	teeth	☐	geese

28

☐	know	☐	hour
☐	no	☐	our
☐	write	☐	son
☐	right	☐	sun

29

☐	anyone	☐	anyhow
☐	anything	☐	anywhere
☐	anybody	☐	anyway
☐	anyplace	☐	anytime

30

☐	someone	☐	somehow
☐	something	☐	somewhere
☐	somebody	☐	sometime
☐	someplace	☐	someday

Words To Review

If you miss a word on your test, write it here. Practice it until you can spell it correctly. Then check the box beside the word.

_____

_____

_____

_____

_____

_____

_____

_____

_____

_____

_____

_____

_____

_____

_____

_____

_____